A Whiteheadian Aesthetic

A WHITEHEADIAN AESTHETIC

Some Implications of Whitehead's Metaphysical Speculation

By DONALD W. SHERBURNE

with a foreword by F. S. C. Northrop

ARCHON BOOKS
1970

SBN: 208 00819 5
Library of Congress Catalog Card Number: 70-103997
Printed in the United States of America

Acknowledgments

WITH the exception of one added chapter and minor revisions, this book is the dissertation submitted in September of 1959 to Yale University in partial fulfillment of the requirements for the degree of Doctor of Philosophy. My debt to the scholarly atmosphere of Yale is great, as is my appreciation to a university which encourages scholarship among its students and junior faculty by such tangible methods as the publishing of this book illustrates.

A book brought out immediately following graduate study inevitably bears the stamp of the many strong personalities who have so recently left their mark on the author. Theodore M. Greene is the only man with whom I have formally studied aesthetics and I am greatly indebted to him for insight and enthusiasm. It is a tribute to the stature of Paul Weiss the philosopher, and the character of Paul Weiss the man, that though he disagrees strongly with many points made in this essay he has nevertheless encouraged me to think my position through and publish the results. Filmer S. C. Northrop and Frederick Fitch both read the original dissertation and urged its publication; I thank them both warmly. Nathaniel Lawrence introduced me to the philosophy of Whitehead and guided my dissertation. Though our discussions rarely bore directly upon the topics I have written about, he has contributed enormously to my development and I am extremely grateful to him, as a person and as a philosopher. His final reading of the Whitehead chapters was exceptionally thorough and relieved the text of many ambiguities and errors.

Ivor Leclerc was spending a leave of absence from Glasgow at Yale when I began this study, and I had the great advantage of reading his book in manuscript at that time. Though I have taken issue with him concerning certain points, I do not want this difference of opinion to obscure the real debt I owe his scholarship and insight. Unfortunately William Christian's comprehensive volume did not appear until after the Whitehead chapters were in final form. He has read sections of my manuscript and offered welcome advice and encouragement.

Nuel D. Belnap, Jr., with whom I shared office space at Yale, provided constant day-to-day stimulation while the manuscript was being written. Although he is making his reputation as a logician, his knowledge of, and interest in, Whitehead's metaphysics is deep. His reading of the Whitehead chapters greatly enhanced their clarity and readability, and his patience in the role of critical sounding board for many of the ideas developed in Part II is deeply appreciated.

An unidentified reader for the Yale Press acutely probed the aesthetic theory; the book is stronger as a result of his suggestions. David Horne, editor for the Yale Press, skillfully guided my manuscript through to publication; I thank him sincerely. Responsibility for inadequacies that remain is mine alone, and I am aware that they exist. Ralph Barton Perry noted that "there are dawning ideas that one would feign take account of, new books that one would feign have read." In the moment of releasing a manuscript to the printer one recognizes the validity of Perry's insight that "philosophy is never finished,—it is only suspended." I offer this book in the spirit of these quotations.

Finally, I acknowledge my greatest debt—to my wife, Elizabeth Darling Sherburne. Without her constant encouragement and efficient handling of a thousand and one details the book could never have been brought into existence. It is fitting that this volume, which explores questions of value and beauty, be dedicated to her.

D<small>ONALD</small> W. S<small>HERBURNE</small>

Nashville, Tennessee
December 1960

Contents

Figures

Foreword

BY F. S. C. NORTHROP

WHITEHEAD's prose is paradoxical. Upon a first reading it seems to be unnecessarily artificial. With later readings, however, one awakes of a sudden with the startling realization that for almost the first time one is observing the facts of experience freshly, directly, and in the concrete.

To read Whitehead with understanding is to realize why. We suppose that we observe directly the data of our experience. In one sense this is true. Obviously we sense what we sense. But human beings are more than their sense organs. Each one of us has an association area in his brain. This area, or more exactly one's introspected imagination which is its correlate, acts upon the aesthetically impressionistic images given by our senses to infer the common sense and scientific objects or persons which the sensory images signify. What we believe we see is, therefore, always the product of the presented, impressionistic images and our habitually conditioned or conscious inferences from them.

To confuse the latter with the former is obviously to commit an error. Kant called this error "dogmatic slumbering." Whitehead calls it the "fallacy of misplaced concreteness" or "the confusion of an entity of thought with a concrete factor of fact."

That this is an error, the reader can check for himself.

Who has not had the experience of seeing the image of a person in the near distance which one believes to be that of one's friend Tom, only to find on closer scrutiny of subsequent images that one has inferred the wrong person and that the successive impressions signify a complete stranger instead. Nor is this a rare occurrence. Any courtroom contains it as a prevalent phenomenon. Whenever several direct witnesses of even a recent event try honestly to describe what they saw, rare indeed is it the case that they do not contradict one another on at least some points about what they "saw." Of course in some cases there may be deliberate liars. But the real difficulty in determining what the law calls the "facts of the case" does not arise solely from the perjurers. Its source also is the failure of the average well-intentioned witness to distinguish with sufficient precision between what he infers from the impressionistic images he senses and the images themselves. Such dogmatic slumbering which produces the fallacy of misplaced concreteness, the legal profession calls the error of mistaken identity.

In any proper courtroom, precisely because this error is so frequent, cross-examination of each witness is required before his testimony is allowed to stand. What a competent cross-examiner does is to shift the attention of the witness, the court and the jury from what the witness says he saw, let us say the defendant Tom Smith, to a more precise description of the images which led him to infer that the person he saw was Tom Smith. If the witness' description of the images is such that they are compatible with its being someone else, then doubt is thrown on the witness' statement of what he "saw." If, on the other hand, the witness describes certain details of the images which are peculiar to the images of Tom Smith, then the effect of the cross-examination is to substantiate rather than to shake his testimony.

Unfortunately most people in arriving at their homemade, amateurish, common-sense scientific and philosophical beliefs are not subject to such cross-examination. The consequence is that they frequently go through life not merely believing that the entities of thought which they have inferred from the concrete events and impressionistic images of their sensuous experience are the concrete facts themselves, but even worse, the inferred entities of thought which they think they see are the result of errors of mistaken identity. Then, under the delusion that they are describing the concrete facts of their experience which the senses give them directly, they have identified both themselves and their universe with nonexistent entities and objects.

In committing this prevalent error, we do more than slander the erroneously identified person and the erroneously interpreted concrete facts of our experience. We also harm ourselves. This self-harm does not arise solely from having made erroneous inferences from the sensed images to the signified entity of thought, thereby quite unintentionally affirming a falsehood while supposing one is merely describing a fact. There is also the harm to oneself which follows inevitably from having cut oneself off aesthetically and emotively from the living water that the human spirit requires for its own refreshment. Robbed thus of the aesthetic, emotive materials of one's own and nature's concrete aesthetic immediacy, one becomes a dull stuffed shirt, prattling bromidic pseudo-moral common-sense platitudes about dead entities of thought that refer to nothing concrete nor to anything verifiably inferable from the concrete. To read Whitehead with care, looking to one's concrete experience rather than to the dull, dead commonplaces of conventional thought, to learn what his words mean, is to give oneself the chance of escaping from this prevalent and unfortunate condition.

Even so, the escape is not easy. For the trouble is in oneself rather than in Whitehead's prose. The confusion of erroneously inferred entities of thought with the concrete colorful events and aesthetically moving impressionistic qualities and continuum of one's immediate experience would not be so prevalent were there not some unconscious, previously conditioned habit of thought in us which has been corrupting both our thinking and our conduct. By going behind the countless abstract nouns in our ordinary language, Whitehead and other competent contemporary students of the relations between words and the sources of their meaning have located one major source of this trouble. It is the subject-predicate grammar of English prose, or any other Aryan language such as Sanskrit, Greek, Latin, French or German, with which quite unconsciously and habitually we think about and describe the concrete facts of our experience. Once this is realized, it becomes evident that it is not Whitehead's prose but ordinary language that is the artificial mode of discourse. Or, to say the same thing positively, it becomes evident that a fresh return to concrete experience will require an unfamiliar terminology to describe what one finds there.

But unless one is to be left with a purely private language which no one else understands, the only language we have for doing this is our ordinary one. At this point the paradox shifts from Whitehead's prose to our own. The very grammar of the sentences we use to give a more correct description of the aesthetically vivid, emotively moving qualities and events of our concrete experience is itself the product of old, erroneously inferred entities of thought. Hence in attempting to correct our corrupted thinking and conduct by writing supposedly clear English sentences which any conventional nitwit who runs can read, we unconsciously and inevitably recorrupt it.

What has to be realized is that this omnipresent corruption is imbedded in our common-sense beliefs, most of our traditional scientific, philosophical, religious, and aesthetic theories and in the discourse and conduct of our literary humanists and of our moralizing and nonmoralizing politicians. It will help us to see how our ordinary language can be modified so as to correct this situation if we use a particular concrete experience to show how English grammar has caused us to describe it falsely and to commit the error of mistaken identity in designating what it signifies.

To be concrete about one's experience one must, at least in the initial stage of its description, be autobiographical: My summers are usually spent in a cottage on a hilltop in New Hampshire, which commands a remarkable view. Frequently I look up to find myself immersed in a panoramic continuum of diversified colors and sensuous forms, never twice the same, which is breath-taking in its immediately experienced natural beauty. If this is not concrete experience, what is? Upon some occasions one portion of this concrete, aesthetic panoramic continuum is to be distinguished from the remainder by an indescribable aesthetic quality to which the English language gives the name "blue."

Were someone who had never experienced this particular concrete object of my senses to ask me what the word "blue" means, neither I nor anyone else could tell him. If he did, however, have in his mind the idea of a material thing or a conscious person one could say negatively that "blue" denotes neither a material thing nor a person. In other words, it is not the kind of factor of knowledge with which either the physicist or the psychologist is primarily concerned. If, however, our inquirer were acquainted with the contemporary impressionistic or abstract art in which concrete factors of fact such as "yellow" are presented in and for themselves without any reference to material objects or persons which they may or may not signify, then we could say to our questioner that "blue" is like this impressionistic painter's "yellow." But this means that the concrete factors of fact which one immediately experiences are essentially and inescapably aesthetic in the sense of the impressionistic artist. Art in this pristine sense of sensuous images, bereft of human inferences beyond them, whether presented breath-takingly upon occasion by nature or created artificially by the impressionistic artist, the writer elsewhere has called "art in its first function." [1] Words referring for their entire meaning to such indescribable, immediately sensed images and experienced items he has called "concepts by intuition," [2] meaning thereby a word and idea which gets its entire meaning from something which is directly sensed, introspected or experienced, and not referring to something such as a table, a chair or Tom Smith that may be correctly or incorrectly inferred from what I immediately sense and experience.

So far in describing my concrete New Hampshirian experience, my English language has not led me astray. But the concrete blues and sensuous shapes which differentiate my breath-taking panoramic continuum of immediacy, signify entities of thought beyond themselves, exactly as the aforementioned impressionistic images signified in fact the presence of a total stranger when one had initially and erroneously inferred that they signified the presence of one's friend Tom.

It is precisely at this point, when I move in thought beyond the bare concrete impressionistic qualities and images of the concrete panoramic continuum that is immediate experience to what they signify, that the subject-predicate grammar of my English prose, or of any other Aryan language, can lead me, as it has led countless scientists, philosophers and people of common sense, into the most serious

1. F. S. C. Northrop, *The Logic of the Sciences and the Humanities* (New York, Macmillan, 1947), chap. 9.
2. Ibid., chap. 5.

errors. For unless I am aware of what the grammar of this language may do to me if I do not watch it most suspiciously, I am likely to describe the "blue" part of my breath-taking panoramic New Hampshire experience by thinking and saying, "The water in Squam Lake is blue." Note what has happened. I have torn the "blue" portion of the all-embracing breath-taking panoramic continuum of concrete aesthetic immediacy away from this continuum, to fasten it to an entity of thought, "The water of Squam Lake," which I infer the "blue" signifies. But similar blues also signify the sky or an oasis in the desert that is not there.

The latter possibility of error is not, however, the most serious danger. By a further experience of images, I can determine whether or not the blue truly signifies "the water of Squam Lake" on this particular occasion. The more serious danger arises when I then walk down through the woods to the lake for a swim and, before plunging in, cup up a handful of its water to observe that it is not blue but clear and colorless. Then if I do not watch most suspiciously the substance-property strait jacket of my English grammatical habit of thought, it is likely to do the following to me, as it has done to Aristotle, St. Thomas, many modern scientists and philosophers, and countless people of common sense: I run the risk, since the blue must be the property of some substance, if the subject-predicate grammar of any Aryan language is to have its way, of saying, "The water of Squam Lake only *appeared* to be blue, when I was in my cottage on the hilltop; it is *really* clear and colorless." Forthwith all the concrete, colorful, breath-taking aesthetic qualities of my concrete experience are torn away from supposedly real things to be assigned to the phantasmic limbo of appearances. Even worse, the entity of thought called a material substance, bereft of consciousness and all emotive or aesthetic qualities, arises in one's mind to be taken not merely as the only real thing in my experience, but also as the initial datum of my experience before I made any inferences from it. In short, one becomes a common-sense materialist with one's feet supposedly on the ground but with one's capacity to either see or make correct inferences from the concrete facts of oneself and nature utterly corrupted and confused. Forthwith artists are regarded as effeminate dilettantes, dealing with ephemeral rather than with real things, and the materialistically minded contemporary Hobbesian lawyers and statesmen, such as Mr. Acheson and the late Mr. Dulles in the free world and the similarly materialistic Marxist Communists who believe that a realistic foreign policy for their own nation in this atomic age can be built on little more than bigger and better hardware, become regarded by the populace as statesmen who are "facing the facts."

But the errors of this patently false description of the concrete facts of experience, into which the subject-predicate grammar has led these common-sense materialists, do not end at this point. For a question immediately arises: If the concretely real is a collection of unconscious, unaesthetic material substances, why does the blue which I saw from the top of the hill exist at all even as an appearance? Again subject-predicate grammar is likely to take over, thereby leading me to infer still another nonexistent entity. This second error of mistaken identity usually takes on the following form: Since every quality must be attached to some substance and since the blue is not a property of the unaesthetic material substances that are "the water of Squam Lake," there must be a different nonmaterial substance to which the blue is attached as its property. Forthwith the additional entity of thought, known supposedly introspectively with direct concreteness and called a conscious or mental substance, is what I "really" saw when I sensed the blue. But immediately even such naïveté notes something to be fishy in one's English prose when one is thus forced to say, "My conscious substantial self is blue." The usual way to get out of this nonsensical predicament in which I have placed myself by using English prose to describe a concrete, breath-taking panoramic aesthetic experience is to retain both the material and the mental substances that this prose has led me erroneously to infer and to then affirm that the blue is the phantasmically projected effect of the action of the material substances upon my private mental substance.

Now the conscious self is stripped of all aesthetic qualities also. Little remains for a person, who thinks of himself in this way, to do but to contemplate his own dull, unaesthetic blank-tablet-ish conscious interior and then utter vacuous moral and religious platitudes about its equally empty spiritual nature. Need one wonder that the power politicians believe that hardware is more trustworthy than such a spirituality and morality?

Nor are the so-called humanists who prattle today about the preciousness and importance of art and the other humanities any better. For what is the discipline that gives them any competence to speak on anything? Clearly it is literature, or, more specifically, the literature of the English or some other Aryan language. Hence this subject-predicate mentality is in them also and in everything that they write. Consequently all they can possibly do is either to talk romantically in an empty way about art as the creative act of such a blank-tablet-ish, essentially unaesthetic, human spirit or else to indulge in discourse about the equally unaesthetic gadgets and techniques of the artist or the media of communication. What there is of significance in any concretely known human being or experience for the artist to say or show, they do not know.

To escape from these errors and confusions by removing the erroneously inferred entities of thought which the subject-predicate grammar of our ordinary language has caused us to foist on ourselves and nature, as if they were the concrete and real facts of our immediate experience, is not easy. More than an expert cross-examiner of what experience witnesses is required. To state what stands up under such cross-examination in our ordinary language without its subject-predicate grammar falsifying the facts of the case in the very statement of them—this is our most difficult problem. Whitehead's method of solving it determined the character of his prose.

When one becomes aware of the fact that one's ordinary language has corrupted the concrete facts of our experience in the very act of stating them only two available procedures are possible: Either (a) one throws away ordinary language to seek in symbolic logic and pure mathematics a symbolism which will not distort the concrete facts of experience and what they correctly signify, or else (b) one keeps ordinary language but introduces technical terms and unconventional usages which minimize its danger of distorting what we see in the very act of stating it. The theoretical mathematical physicist uses the first of these two procedures, often supplementing it with the second. Every competent contemporary philosopher uses the second procedure, checking it by appeal to the first. Whitehead's competence as a mathematician, symbolic logician, and philosophical analyst of concrete experience was such that in his different articles and books he used both methods. It is likely that one of the mathematical possibles listed in his earlier 1905 paper, "On Mathematical Concepts of the Material World," [3] is the metaphysical system which was stated in his technically modified English prose in *Process and Reality*.

Each procedure has its advantages and disadvantages.

3. F. S. C. Northrop, and Mason W. Gross, *Alfred North Whitehead: An Anthology* (Cambridge University Press, 1953; New York, Macmillan, 1953), pp. 13–82.

Hence both must be used. Because symbolic logic and mathematics deal with the possible relational structures of all possible conceivable worlds, their language, if properly chosen, can fit itself to any concrete experience and what it correctly signifies as tested empirically without risk of distortion. The danger is thereby escaped of forcing the particular facts of concrete aesthetic immediacy into the Procrustean bed of the subject-predicate grammar of Aryan linguistic prose. The disadvantages of a complete symbolic logical and mathematical language are, however, twofold. First, as is obvious, it does not have the wide popular appeal and reach of ordinary prose. Second, its entity terms are always variables. This means that one must go outside the mathematical symbolism to the material constants which are the values of its variables and to some but not all of the nonmathematical concepts of ordinary prose, those namely which the writer, just above, called "concepts by intuition." This appeal to the concepts by intuition of ordinary prose, e.g., to words such as "blue" in the sense used earlier, is necessary in order to correlate the unobservable entity variables and their many-termed relations, designated by the mathematically expressed postulates or axioms, with the concrete data of concrete experience. Otherwise the mathematically expressed statement of the concrete facts of our experience and what they signify could not be verified as being the correct one.

Since the concrete data denoted by concepts by intuition require the symbols of ordinary language for their statement, the problem becomes that of preserving the latter words in ordinary language, such as blue, while eliminating the distortions of concrete experience and the erroneously inferred entities of thought entailed by its two-termed subject-predicate grammar.

The reason why mathematics and particularly its symbolic logic of relations are required to show us how to do this is easy to understand and applies as much to the reader's ordinary facts of his immediate experience as to the more technical experimentally determined facts of mathematical physics. Expressed mathematically in terms of the logic of relations, the reason is that any concrete sensed property such as "blue" or "hot" is a function of many variables and not, as subject-predicate grammar supposes, of merely one, namely, the substance of which it is supposed to be a predicate. Once this is realized, the need to find either an unaesthetic material substance or an unaesthetic mental substance to which to fasten the blue which I sensed vanishes; also the necessity of throwing aesthetic immediacy out of oneself and nature vanishes along with it.

But since ordinary prose requires one to fasten every property to some subject term, how can one express in this prose the concrete fact that the blue which I directly sense is a function of many variables, i.e. whether the sun is shining, whether there are clouds in the sky, where I am located when I sense it and many other factors. The answer, and this is the answer which Whitehead gives, is by making the subject of the English sentence not a substance, but a many-termed relation of which the blue is but one of the terms. This has the effect of stating in English prose that the blue is not the property of a substance, i.e. it is not a function of only one variable, but is instead a function of many variables designating several other facts of concrete experience and what they signify. This is the point of the thesis of Chapter VII in *The Concept of Nature* which, more than any other, is, in this writer's judgment, the key to Whitehead's entire philosophy. This key thesis is that sense objects such as blue "ingress" into nature in many-termed relations. An example of such ingression, similar to my concrete New Hampshirian example, he describes as follows: "The sense-awareness of the blue as situated in a certain event which I call the situation, is . . . exhibited as the sense-awareness of a relation between the blue, the percipient event of the observer, the situation, and intervening events." [4]

When he commented to me on his use of the somewhat unfamiliar word "ingression" to describe this many-termed relation between the concretely sensed blue and other concrete entities and events of our experience soon after he had written it in the early 1920's, he said that he chose this word for two reasons: First, in the hope that its unfamiliarity would shock the reader out of his habit of supposing that the qualities we directly sense are related to other facts of concrete experience by the two-termed relation of predicate of a substance. Second, because the ambiguity of the word "ingression" leaves open, exactly as does any concrete experience, the precise many-termed relation and its many terms upon which the existence of the "blue" as a concrete fact of nature depends for its existence in a particular occasion and situation. This is for future images and occasions to determine. Forthwith the real world is the aesthetically breath-taking colorful world and it is no longer necessary to infer nonexistent, unaesthetic material and mental substances whose interaction has the effect of throwing our emotive, aesthetic selves and the other directly sensed concrete facts of experience out of nature as unreal phantasms. The aesthetic implications are obvious. In *Process and Reality* a noun is selected to denote this many-termed relational ingression of any concrete factor of fact into the totality of concrete facts and what they signify. This noun is Nexus.

The procedure should now be clear for solving the linguistic paradox of using ordinary language to correct its distortions of what it tries to say. This procedure consists in retaining its concepts by intuition such as "blue" or

4. Alfred North Whitehead, *The Concept of Nature* (Cambridge University Press, 1920), p. 152.

"painful" in their ordinary meaning while also using other words in a technical way which is in part their ordinary meaning and in part a novel meaning. This is what Kant did. It is what Whitehead has done. It is what the writer attempted to do with his expressions "the differentiated aesthetic continuum" and "the undifferentiated aesthetic continuum." [5] These are all attempts to direct attention back from the old erroneously inferred entities of thought to the concrete inescapably aesthetic and moral data of our immediate experience.

It may be noted parenthetically that the contemporary European existentialists' attempt to shift attention from what they call the *Sein* (of entities of thought) to the here-now-Da-ness of this Sein in concrete human experiences and concerns is a linguistically confused and romantically irresponsible attempt in the same direction. It is confused because, neglectful of the logic of many-termed relations, it is dominated still by the subject-predicate thing-language. It is romantically irresponsible because surreptitiously it is still under the obsession of the pseudo-creativity of self-sufficient mental substances or spirits, a creativity which is pseudo precisely because the spiritual consciousness from which it proceeds is either a vacuous blank tablet or an arbitrary Fichtean will with no relational norms whatever to guide it.

Having, after the manner of Whitehead, in a linguistically clear and empirically responsible way, rid ourselves of the old erroneously inferred entities of thought and having returned to concrete immediacy to find its aesthetically vivid and breath-taking events, the realities rather than the phantasmic ephemeral projections of ourselves and our world, we are in a position to pass to the more correctly inferred

5. F. S. C. Northrop, *The Meeting of East and West* (New York, Macmillan, 1946), pp. 303–11, 335 ff.

entities of thought which these concrete realities signify. These signified entities in their lawful, many-termed relations to the concrete will provide their novel criterion of the beautiful. The significance of recent impressionistic and abstract art is that, like Whitehead in his earlier *Principles of Natural Knowledge* and *The Concept of Nature*, it has, in its return to the impressionistic images and continuum of concrete immediacy, broken us and art free from the old Euclidian proportions and perspectives and other old entities of thought and theology which in major part defined the traditional classical concept of the beautiful.

But, as Whitehead also realized, these inescapably aesthetic concrete particulars signify objects and meanings beyond themselves, even though these objects and meanings are not the traditional erroneously inferred entities of thought which in such major part made the classical concept of the beautiful what it was. Moreover, as he noted, the persisting objects and meanings project themselves back into the particular aesthetic occasions of concrete immediacy. It is this concept of the beautiful identified not with concrete aesthetic immediacy *per se* but with what it signifies, which the writer had in mind when he spoke of "art in its second function." [6] Whitehead's specification of the categories that define the beautiful in this second, fuller and novel sense of what the concrete signifies was implicit in his earlier works on the philosophy of natural knowledge and mathematical physics. It was partially articulated in the two chapters on "Abstraction" and "God" in *Science and the Modern World* and further articulated in *Religion in the Making*. The first systematic summary and statement occurred, however, in his major work, *Process and Reality*. Some of the aesthetic implications of the latter work have been in-

6. Northrop, *The Logic of the Sciences and the Humanities*, chap. 9, note 1, previously in *Furioso*, Vol. 1, No. 4, 1941.

dicated recently by Mary A. Wyman in her book, *The Lure for Feeling*,[7] the title of which is a phrase of Whitehead's.

Notwithstanding the indubitably aesthetic character of Whitehead's account of both concrete experience and what it signifies, he never wrote a book on aesthetics. Perhaps the reason was that he believed that he had already done so in the books that he did write.

Whether this be the explanation, I do not know. I do know, however, that in the early 1920's when he took me page by page and chapter by chapter through *The Principles of Natural Knowledge* and *The Concept of Nature*, he often stopped to point out the aesthetic character of the concrete facts from which all science, philosophy and reflection take their inception. Upon one occasion he added that, unless one finds something aesthetic in the concrete facts from which anyone starts his knowledge, be he philosopher, scientist or man of common sense, he will never come out at the end of his reflections with an adequate theory of art.

Whatever may be the reason why Whitehead did not write a book in which art was his major concern, we are in a position now to interpret the importance of the present book by Professor Sherburne. It is an attempt to answer one question: If Whitehead had written the book on aesthetics which is implicit in the books that he did write, what would this book be?

The results speak for themselves. We may perhaps best describe these results in the way in which Plato described his own cosmological theory in his *Timaeus*. If this is not Whitehead's book on aesthetics, then it is at least very much like it. Some of us, however, who have spent decades in the study of and reflection upon Whitehead's work, be-

7. Mary A. Wyman, *The Lure for Feeling*, New York, Philosophical Library, 1960.

lieve that Professor Sherburne has done even more than give a documented and reasonable answer to the foregoing important question. For, by illuminating certain of Whitehead's abstract distinctions and categories by means of particular aesthetic materials, he has given us not merely a richer and Whiteheadian kind of understanding of art, but also a deeper insight into Whitehead's very concrete, most original, subtle and systematic philosophy.

Abbreviations

All page references to Whitehead's works are to the American editions, published by the Macmillan Company, with the exception of PNK and RM, where the Cambridge editions are cited, and FR, where the pagination of the Beacon Press paperback edition is followed. Special permission to quote extended passages from Whitehead has been granted by the Macmillan Company and the Cambridge University Press.

AI	*Adventures of Ideas,*	1933
FR	*The Function of Reason,*	1929
MT	*Modes of Thought,*	1938
PNK	*The Principles of Natural Knowledge,*	1919
PR	*Process and Reality,*	1929
RM	*Religion in the Making,*	1926
SMW	*Science and the Modern World,*	1925

Part I

SYSTEMATIC FRAMEWORK

1. Introduction

THIS is primarily an essay in aesthetic theory, but since it assumes that clarity and precision in aesthetic discourse are achieved only when the central concepts involved are firmly grounded in a metaphysical system, it also seeks to examine the general adequacy of a particular metaphysical system by testing the ability of that system to generate fruitful aesthetic analysis. The system under investigation is that of Alfred North Whitehead. I shall suggest some of the implications for aesthetics of the process approach to philosophy as that approach is exemplified in Whitehead's mature metaphysical speculation.

I do not consider aesthetic problems until Chapter 5. Clarification of this procedure is crucial; otherwise the reader may feel that he has two books: one about Whitehead and one about aesthetics.

In examining the language of religious expression Whitehead writes: "it is impossible to fix the sense of fundamental terms except by reference to some definite metaphysical way of conceiving the most penetrating description of the universe." As an example he warns that "in expressing our conception of God, words such as 'personal' and 'impersonal,' 'entity,' 'individuality,' 'actual,' require the closest careful watching, lest in different connections we should use them in different senses, not to speak of the danger of failing to use them in any determinate sense" (RM 66). It is my contention that the fundamental terms of aesthetic

3

analysis require the same "fixing" in order to avoid the same dangers. Such notions as "aesthetic experience," "artistic creation," and "aesthetic object" need their senses fixed by reference to a systematic interpretation of reality. The reason, then, why four chapters of detailed analysis of certain aspects of Whitehead's metaphysics precede the chapters dealing with aesthetic problems is that without the understanding of Whitehead's categories as laid out in these four chapters one cannot grasp the significance of the manner in which the aesthetic analysis of the later chapters emerges naturally from Whitehead's brilliant speculative account of the nature of things and acquires clarity and precision as a result of its dependence on that account.

Also, the presupposition of my study is that clarity and precision in aesthetic discourse is achieved only when the central concepts involved are firmly grounded in a metaphysical theory. When successfully completed, therefore, the aesthetic theory will reflect back in an important manner upon the metaphysical system from which it originates. As Susanne Langer says:

> A philosophical theory is not called upon to furnish "irrefutable proofs," but concepts that give rise to insight and discovery. One can sometimes prove the consistency of concepts, and inconsistency can always be logically demonstrated; but one cannot prove the excellence of a concept, even if it be logically impeccable, except pragmatically, by operating with it successfully.[1]

Part II of this book is an attempt to operate with Whitehead's categories, and to the extent that it operates successfully with them it demonstrates their excellence. White-

1. *Reflections on Art* (Baltimore, Johns Hopkins University Press, 1958), p. xii.

head has noted that a "philosophical scheme should be coherent, logical, and, in respect to its interpretation, applicable and adequate. Here 'applicable' means that some items of experience are thus interpretable, and 'adequate' means that there are no items incapable of such interpretation" (PR 4). By showing that aesthetic experience is interpretable within this philosophical scheme, applicability is satisfied and adequacy has been extended over another dimension of experience. Success in operating pragmatically with the concepts of a scheme provides the sort of "proof" of their excellence that it is possible to give. Therefore, by presenting evidence that it is fruitful to conduct investigations into the problems of aesthetics from within the framework of Whitehead's metaphysics, Part II will contribute evidence for the adequacy of that metaphysics, thereby strengthening the appeal of Whitehead's philosophy. In this way the aesthetic theory reflects back upon the metaphysical system from which it originates, and the book acquires an additional unifying factor.

Clarification of the relationship between my own chapters on aesthetics and Whitehead's writings may be useful. It should be understood at the outset that Part II is not a systematic compilation of Whitehead's scattered remarks about art and aesthetics. It is, rather, my own creative attempt to *use* Whitehead's metaphysical categories in framing an original way of approaching aesthetic problems. Although Whitehead utilizes the language of aesthetics and his own aesthetic experience in shaping his basic metaphysical categories, he does very little to indicate how these categories are applied to the specific problems of aesthetics. The most important exception occurs in Part IV of *Adventures of Ideas*, where he addresses himself directly to a definition of beauty. Victor Lowe has noted that, "Whitehead now [in *Adventures of Ideas*], by defining *beauty* in terms of his metaphysics, repays the debt which his systematic thought owed to that part of its 'humanistic' background." [2] I am suggesting that here Whitehead is repaying only a small part of the debt. What is repaid is repaid well, and I count it a favorable mark for my own theory that in section v of Chapter 7 Whitehead's account of beauty fits neatly the total theory which is Part II of this book. But a definition of beauty is not the whole of an aesthetic theory; [3] the philosopher seeking to understand the arts is also concerned with, among other things, understanding aesthetic experience, artistic creation, the ontological status of the work of art, the function of art, and the sense in which truth is a notion relevant to art. There are other problems the aesthetician concerns himself with, but these are the ones I have singled out in considering only *some* of the implications for aesthetics of

2. "Whitehead's Philosophical Development," in *The Philosophy of Alfred North Whitehead*, ed. Paul A. Schilpp (2d ed. New York, Tudor Publishing Co., 1951), p. 118.

3. It is true, of course, that many philosophers have wanted to restrict aesthetics to the single task of defining beauty. In pointing this out Thomas Munro (*Towards Science in Aesthetics*, New York, Liberal Arts Press, 1956, p. 140) has cited the following definition of *esthétique* which appeared as recently as 1947 in André Lalande's *Vocabulaire technique et critique de la philosophie* (Paris): "Science ayant pour objet le jugement d'appréciation en tant qu'il s'applique à la distinction du Beau et du Laid" (The science having for its object value judgments insofar as they discriminate between the beautiful and the ugly). Munro goes on to note (p. 262): "To define 'the beautiful' correctly, and give a true account of its nature and criteria, was commonly regarded as the sole or central task of aesthetics. . . . The concept no longer holds a central, preeminent position in aesthetics as a whole. . . . Some of the reasons are obvious. Aesthetics . . . has become aware of the great diversity and scope of the phenomena which it has to investigate, and of the need for a complex apparatus of terms to describe and interrelate them. The single concept of beauty, along with a few other traditional 'aesthetic categories,' such as the ugly, sublime, and pretty, seem quite inadequate to do so . . ." One might, by using "aesthetics" in its narrow sense, conclude that in defining beauty Whitehead has worked out the implications for aesthetics of his metaphysical speculation. It is my contention that in the broader, today more generally accepted, sense of the term Whitehead has not himself worked out the implications for aesthetics of his metaphysical system. This I attempt to do in Part II, below.

Whitehead's mature metaphysical speculation. And in these areas Whitehead provides very little guidance, usually because he doesn't consider the problem, or sometimes, as in the case of his scattered comments on the function of art, because what he does say doesn't seem to me to be either profound or suggestive. Whitehead himself calls for this application of his metaphysics: "it must be one of the motives of a complete cosmology, to construct a system of ideas which bring[s] the aesthetic, moral, and religious interests into relation with those concepts of the world which have their origin in natural science" (PR vi). Whitehead himself, in *Religion in the Making*, has brought the religious interests into relation with his metaphysical concepts. Edmund Jabez Thompson has brought the moral interests into relation with Whitehead's concepts.[4] I will attempt to bring the aesthetic interests into relation with Whitehead's concepts.

Part I of this book is essentially an introduction to the aesthetic theory of Part II. Yet in reading Whitehead with the explicit purpose of discovering in his categories the foundation for a suggestive, interesting, and adequate aesthetic theory, I found myself preparing materials which are of intrinsic interest simply as interpretations and clarifications of his thought. Throughout Part I, I have interspersed anticipations of how the metaphysical notions being considered will generate aesthetic insights, but I hope, nevertheless, that Part I can stand on its own feet as a study of certain limited aspects of Whitehead's system—though these are, of course, aspects relevant to the subsequent aesthetic analysis. Two aims, then, have dictated the organization of Part I. First, it was essential to describe the crucial notions that appear later. Secondly, it was important that these notions not simply be exhibited in isolation but that they be presented as integral parts of a system, so that the

4. *An Analysis of the Thought of Whitehead and Hocking Concerning Good and Evil*, Chicago, University of Chicago Press, 1935.

aesthetic theory of Part II could be seen to evolve naturally and logically from a comprehensive metaphysical system which purports to specify those general ideas in terms of which all that is real is analyzable. Part I is consequently a systematic introduction to Whitehead's thought.

I have said that, given the four criteria of excellence by which a metaphysical system can be evaluated—coherence, logicality, applicability, and adequacy—this book should primarily strengthen the two empirical tests, applicability and adequacy. Yet Part I is relevant to the rational criteria of coherence and logicality. Some commentators have argued that Whitehead's metaphysics suffers from deep-seated inconsistencies that vitiate its metaphysical usefulness. While prepared to grant that Whitehead's system undoubtedly requires many modifications, I feel that the system is so pregnant with suggestions for further applications in various areas of human experience that in several instances where I have been able to refute attempts to demonstrate inconsistency I have done so in the hope that these refutations will give the Cassandras pause and at the same time encourage further attempts to rework the Whiteheadian categories, where needed, in an effort to achieve maximum coherence as an ever firmer foundation for demonstrated applicability. In my own broadening of the notion of transmutation to cover two distinct species, horizontal and vertical, I have undertaken one such limited modification of the categoreal scheme.

The thesis defended in these pages, then, is that the ability of Whitehead's system to generate fruitful concepts for aesthetic analysis contributes substantially to a verification of the claim, made by Whitehead, that his system is applicable and adequate as well as coherent and logical. This thesis ties together the two parts of the book and makes it, I hope, something more than an essay in aesthetic theory, though this it remains primarily.

2. The Formative Elements

THE concept of an actual entity—or, equivalently,[1] an actual occasion, or a creature—is at the heart of Whitehead's metaphysical system. Actual entities are the locus of the fullness of being; they are what is really real. Actual entities are the locus of agency. It is a basic tenet of Whitehead's system "that there is no agency in abstraction from actual occasions, and that existence involves implication in agency" (AI 379). An actual occasion is not to be abstracted into something apart from, behind, or containing its agency. It *is* its agency, or process; its very being is constituted by its process, its becoming. No process, no existence; and apart from actual entities there is no process. This is the ontological principle.[2]

For purposes of analysis, but these purposes only, the process that is the becoming of an actual occasion can be divided into phases. Chapter 3 will analyze the phases of the becoming of an actual occasion. The present chapter will systematically explore three key concepts in Whitehead's

1. The unique exception to this equivalence is the actual entity, God, who is distinguished by Whitehead from the temporal actual entities. At PR 135 he writes: "In the subsequent discussion, 'actual entity' will be taken to mean a conditioned actual entity of the temporal world, unless God is expressly included in the discussion. The term 'actual occasion' will always exclude God from its scope." He also notes, PR 119, that "the term 'actual occasion' is used synonomously with 'actual entity'; but chiefly when its character of extensiveness has some direct relevance to the discussion . . ."

2. See PR 27–28, 36–37.

system presupposed by the notion of an actual occasion. These three concepts, referred to by Whitehead as the formative elements,[3] are creativity, eternal objects, and God. It should be understood that an exhaustive account of these formative elements will not be attempted; only the aspects of each which are presupposed by Chapter 3 and which provide a foundation for the aesthetic theory to be developed later can be touched on in this brief introduction to Whitehead's system. Creativity will be the first element considered.

1. CREATIVITY

My analysis of Whitehead's doctrine of creativity is important as an introduction to the aesthetic theory of Part II. I begin with T. E. Hulme's summary of an aspect of Bergson's thought that is relevant:

> To use the metaphor which one is by now so familiar with—the stream of the inner life, and the definite crystallised shapes on the surface—the big artist, the creative artist, the innovator, leaves the level where things are crystallised out into these definite shapes, and, diving down into the inner flux, comes back with a new shape which he endeavors to fix.[4]

The "crystallised shapes on the surface" are, of course, rational structures, and artistic creation is, for Bergson, a movement beyond such structures. I take very seriously Whitehead's remark, made in connection with Bergson, James, and Dewey: "One of my preoccupations has been to rescue their type of thought from the charge of anti-intellectualism, which rightly or wrongly has been associated with it" (PR vii). An indispensable step in effecting this

3. See RM 77–78.
4. *Speculations: Essays on Humanism and the Philosophy of Art* (New York, Harcourt, Brace, and London, Routledge, Kegan Paul, 1924), p. 149.

"rescue" is the rationalization of "the inner flux," the giving to it of an intelligible structure. This Whitehead does in terms of his doctrine of creativity. Chapter 3 of this book will examine in detail Whitehead's genetic analysis of conscious intellection, an analysis following from the doctrine of creativity, and Chapter 8 will present a theory of artistic creation based on, not opposed to, that analysis of conscious intellection and the components on which it depends. Consequently, the aesthetic theory that emerges from Whitehead's process philosophy is very different from that which emerges from Bergson's process philosophy. An understanding of the nature of creativity is, then, crucial not only for an understanding of Whitehead's metaphysics but also for insight into the aesthetic theory that can be drawn out of his categories.

I will preface my own account of Whitehead's doctrine of creativity with a brief summary of Ivor Leclerc's introduction to and interpretation of this notion. Leclerc is especially helpful, since he neatly relates Whitehead to traditional philosophical positions while introducing the notion of creativity. Yet his account needs extensive supplementation before a clear picture emerges of how Whitehead is refining the Bergsonian doctrine of flux.

Leclerc's approach to the problem of creativity begins with an identification of the category of "actual entity" with the traditional concept of οὐσία, "*that* which is." Tracing Leclerc's main arguments will introduce the concept of an actual occasion and reveal the sense in which this concept presupposes creativity as a formative element.[5]

Since each particular rendering of "*that* which is"—be it

5. I summarize below a few points from pp. 53–90 of Ivor Leclerc's *Whitehead's Metaphysics: An Introductory Exposition*, New York, Macmillan, and London, Allen and Unwin, 1958. These pages provide an excellent entry into Whitehead's thought.

"substance," "monad," or "actual entity"—bears within the context of its particular philosophical system the secondary connotation of *"what* that is which is," Leclerc undertakes a painstaking, step-by-step analysis of how Whitehead determined *what* his οὐσία would be by studying the great traditional answers to this question. For present purposes three conclusions from this analysis need to be noted.

In the first place, *"that* which is" cannot be "one" but must be "many"; Whitehead rejects metaphysical monism on the grounds that a monistic system must be either utterly inapplicable, as is that of Parmenides, or else incoherent, since to account for change it must introduce something like Spinozistic modes, the existence of which is quite arbitrarily disconnected from any necessity for differentiation arising out of the one really real substance.[6] Secondly, *"that* which is" must be *causa sui;* Descartes has correctly written, Leclerc notes, that "the conservation of a substance, in each moment of its duration, requires the same power and act that would be necessary to create it, supposing it were not yet in existence . . ."[7] Whitehead sees that ultimately something in a philosophical system must be *causa sui* if an infinite regress is to be avoided, but instead of assigning this characteristic to God alone, he assigns it to each of the actual entities. Thirdly, although each of the actual entities is consequently the locus of "power," or "act" (hence the designation *"act*ual entity"), each is also an *entity.*[8] Zeno has demonstrated that there can be no continuity of becoming, so actual entities are epochal drops of process, individual units of becoming "in each of which the process of becoming is completed . . . Each is a process of becoming distinct from the others."[9] But Zeno's

6. Ibid., pp. 53–59.
7. From Descartes' Third Meditation; quoted ibid., p. 65.
8. Ibid., pp. 71–78.
9. Ibid., p. 74.

argument could still be brought to bear on each individual occasion, and this procedure Whitehead forestalls by arguing

> that in every act of becoming there is the becoming of something with temporal extension; but that the act itself is not extensive, in the sense that it is divisible into earlier and later acts of becoming which correspond to the extensive divisibility of what has become. [PR 107]

This is the doctrine "that the creature is extensive, but that its act of becoming is not extensive" (PR 107) and is avowedly based on William James' insight that "Your acquaintance with reality grows literally by buds or drops of perception. Intellectually and on reflection you can divide these into components, but as immediately given, they come totally or not at all." [10]

To summarize these points, that which is, the really real, is many; there are many actual entities varying in importance but sharing certain generic principles. Each of these *act*ualities is *causa sui*, is the locus of power, or *act*. But each is also an entity, an individual unit of becoming which, though extensive and hence divi*sible*, is not therefore necessarily divi*ded*: "the atomic actuality is 'extensive' by virtue of its process of becoming, but that process of becoming is itself one 'epochal whole' . . ." [11]

This all too brief description of Whitehead's category of actual entity, by showing in certain respects *what* that is which really is, prepares the way for a discussion of creativity as a formative element presupposed by the category of actual entity.

Given this initial description, creativity can be viewed as

10. Quoted from chap. 10 of James' *Some Problems of Philosophy*, at PR 105–6.
11. Leclerc, p. 77.

a notion necessary for avoiding incoherence. Incoherence is the arbitrary disconnection of first principles, and it has already been shown that Whitehead feels strongly that a monistic ontology must be either inapplicable, as is that of Parmenides, or else incoherent as a result of introducing something like Spinozistic modes in order to account for change. The incoherence here would arise because the modes, as principles, are quite arbitrarily disconnected from any necessity in the one really real substance for differentiating itself into modes; they follow from no such necessity but simply from the need for philosophers to account for change. Whitehead's pluralism enables him to avoid this sort of incoherence, which I shall refer to as *vertical* incoherence, because he has attributed "act," or "power" to each actual entity, so that there is no reason to appeal to a really real, superior substance to sustain actual entities.

But perhaps there may be another kind of incoherence that threatens Whitehead at this point. He has insisted that in each actual entity the process of becoming is completed, but is, however, committed in his system to an everlasting on-goingness of succeeding actual occasions. The question is, does not this commitment involve what I shall refer to as *horizontal* incoherence? Does not the epochal theory of actuality fail to provide a coherent reason, i.e. a reason inherent in its own first principles, why any given actual occasion must be succeeded by a fresh actual occasion in order that the universe not lose its dynamic character and become static, evaporating without trace as would an uncommunicated dream were the dreamer suddenly annihilated? This is meant to be a rhetorical question, for Whitehead does not avoid vertical incoherence only to slip into horizontal incoherence. It is asked because if one sees how Whitehead avoids horizontal incoherence, one understands the concept of creativity, and vice versa.

Leclerc recognizes this point. Though he does not set

up his discussion of creativity in terms of horizontal incoherence as I have done, he concludes his analysis of creativity with the remark (p. 87) that "thus is secured the character of the universe to be perpetually 'going on'," in effect saying that Whitehead's system is not horizontally incoherent. I shall summarize Leclerc's remarks on creativity, then suggest a misleading impression those remarks are apt to give, and finally present my own exposition of what I find to be crucial in Whitehead's doctrine of creativity.

Leclerc writes:

> Whitehead therefore conceives a multiplicity of actualities, each being or existing as a 'process of becoming' by virtue of its own activity. Each individual actuality *is* (i.e. exists as) an 'act of becoming', and each act *becomes* an individual actual entity. That is, each individual actuality arises out of a process of activity which is generic to all. Each activity is thus an individualization of the ultimate generic activity. In other words, each actuality constitutes a particular individual form taken by the generic activity.
>
> In saying this it is implied that there is no 'activity' as such apart from the activity of the individual actualities, in the same sense as, in a materialistic theory, there is no 'matter' apart from the individual actual entities . . .[12]

The "ultimate generic activity" here referred to is creativity. Creativity is an ultimate which exists only in its individual instances. Leclerc quotes Whitehead's well-known passage: "In all philosophical theory there is an ultimate which is actual in virtue of its accidents. It is only then capable of characterization through its accidental embodiments, and apart from these accidents is devoid of

12. Ibid., p. 82.

actuality." [13] Leclerc summarizes the essence of the doctrine:

> What is requisite, Whitehead maintains, is to recognize the 'ultimate' without denying actuality to the individualizations of the ultimate. In his doctrine the 'ultimate' is not conceived as itself an *actual* entity: it is the basic activity of self-creation generic to all individual actual entities. That is to say, it is the generic activity conceived in abstraction from the individual instantiations of that activity. This 'ultimate', this generic activity of self-creation, Whitehead terms 'creativity'.[14]

This is an excellent summary statement of Whitehead's doctrine, but in its brevity it is puzzling and paradoxical. Leclerc recognizes that creativity as he has described it is "ultimate" in two senses: " 'Creativity' is therefore 'ultimate' in the sense, first, that it constitutes the generic metaphysical character of all actualities; and secondly it is the 'ultimate' in the sense that the actualities are individualizations of it" (p. 86). In the first sense creativity is an abstraction of a common activity of the individual actualities; in the second sense creativity is, however, "not merely a common feature of the individual actual entities," but "an 'ultimate' instantiated in individual actualities, and of which the individual actualities are instances" (p. 86). In this second sense Leclerc speaks of creativity as "transcending each *individual* actual creature . . . [although] not itself actual" (p. 87).

The crucial problem is to provide a meaning for the term "transcending" in this second sense (in which creativity is ultimate) which is compatible with the first, ab-

---

13. Ibid., p. 83. Whitehead continues in this passage (PR 10–11): "In the philosophy of organism this ultimate is termed 'creativity' . . ."
14. Leclerc, p. 84.

straction-of-a-common-activity, sense (in which creativity is ultimate). Leclerc is aware of the need to get the two senses in which creativity is the ultimate together in one harmonious theory.

> There is a certain difficulty, however, in achieving a clear and consistent conception of the 'ultimate'. If we concentrate on the individual actualities, there appear to be only the actualities, with perhaps some discernable common feature. . . .
>
> If, on the other hand, we concentrate on the 'ultimate', there is a strong tendency to conceive it as itself 'actual', as somehow 'more real' than the individual embodiments, the outcome being the adoption of a monistic theory. [p. 83]

The second alternative appears to throw one back dangerously close to a monistic theory, as Leclerc notes, and since Whitehead is convinced that monism is incoherent, this alternative might seem to invite vertical incoherence. But the first alternative leaves the system open to the charge of horizontal incoherence, because it then appears that there is no reason inherent in the first principles why there should be an everlasting on-goingness of succeeding actual occasions. The sobering thought occurs that the philosophy of organism might be caught in a dilemma where it can only avoid horizontal incoherence to the extent that it invokes vertical incoherence, and vice versa. Unless some point between these two alternatives can be found to "concentrate on," Whitehead's system seems to be in serious trouble.

The system, of course, is not in trouble here. The key notion which must be understood is the notion of "transcending"; when Whitehead's full meaning is grasped, "transcending" acquires a concrete meaning that enables the doctrine of creativity to avoid both horizontal and

vertical incoherence. The weakness of Leclerc's analysis is
the failure to elucidate what is meant by this crucial notion of "transcending"—which is why his conclusion is
both correct and unsatisfying. Whitehead achieves coherence, he writes (p. 87),

> by conceiving the 'ultimate' as 'creativity', a universal
> process of creative activity which, while transcending
> each *individual* actual creature, is not itself actual, but
> is instantiated in the individual actualities. Thus is
> secured the conception of a connected 'universe'. And
> thus is secured the character of the universe to be
> perpetually 'going on': for its 'ultimate' character is
> that of self-creating activity. The individual actual
> entities are the 'creatures' of this universal 'creativity'.
> They are not creatures of creativity in the sense that
> creativity is a 'creator', i.e. in the sense that 'creativity'
> is itself a transcendent actuality creating them; but
> in the sense that the 'ultimate', creativity, individual-
> izes itself in the individual creatures.

This statement is correct but unsatisfying because the
sense of "transcending" which makes it right is not specified
and a reader not thoroughly familiar with *Process and
Reality* is undoubtedly at a loss, given Leclerc's account, to
understand how it is possible that creativity "transcends"
but doesn't really become "transcendent." In the remaining
paragraphs of this section I shall specify the sense of "transcends" which fills out Leclerc's account of creativity. This
clarification will also indicate how Whitehead refines,
rationalizes, the Bergsonian doctrine of flux.

This analysis consists primarily of unpacking the tremendously compact passages that constitute Whitehead's
description of the Category of the Ultimate (PR 31–32).
He begins that description with a crucial paragraph.

'Creativity,' 'many,' 'one' are the ultimate notions involved in the meaning of the synonymous terms 'thing,' 'being,' 'entity.' These three notions complete the Category of the Ultimate and are presupposed in all the more special categories. [PR 31]

The ultimate is not a thing, or an entity; it is a cluster of three notions, only one of which is creativity, in terms of which "thinghood" is itself an intelligible notion. Neither is creativity a thing or an entity; it is a principle, a characterization of ultimate matter of fact.[15] It expresses the relationship between "one" and "many." It expresses the relationship in virtue of which "the term 'many' presupposes the term 'one,' and the term 'one' presupposes the term 'many'" (PR 31).

In the first instance creativity is the principle of concrete togetherness. Creativity "is that ultimate principle by which the many, which are the universe disjunctively, become the one actual occasion, which is the universe conjunctively" (PR 31). Whitehead describes this principle more simply: "It lies in the nature of things that the many enter into complex unity" (PR 31). The universe abhors a many; it is just an ultimate fact that the universe cannot tolerate a disjunctive diversity.

In the second instance creativity is the principle of novelty. It is the principle that "An actual occasion is a novel entity diverse from any entity in the 'many' which it unifies" (PR 31). As the principle of novelty, creativity guarantees that the entity which emerges from the concrescing activity whereby the universe overcomes its abhorrence of a "many" is itself "a novel entity, disjunctively among the many entities which it synthesizes" (PR 32). Thus to as-

---

15. "The category [Category] of the Ultimate expresses the general principle presupposed in the three more special categories [of Existence, of Explanation, and of Categoreal Obligations]" (PR 31).

suage the abhorrence of a "many" is to introduce a disjunctive diversity into the universe once more. Each actual occasion draws into a one, a unity, the disjunction of diverse elements in the universe. But in so doing, each unifying concrescence becomes itself, as a unity, a disjunctive element over against the elements it has unified: it has increased the disjunction by one. In this sequence is contained the basic rhythm of process. On-goingness is assured; to assuage is to create the conditions demanding assuagement. The very process which eliminates disjunctive diversity is productive of disjunctive diversity, and the universe cannot tolerate disjunctive diversity. The alternation between "many" and "one" and "one" and "many" is everlasting.

Given the ultimate notions "many" and "one," the third ultimate notion, "creativity," relates the other two in a manner productive of the pulsations of process which are the actual entities of Whitehead's system. "There is a rhythm of process whereby creation produces natural pulsation, each pulsation forming a natural unit of historic fact" (MT 120). The pulsations are the entities; the three notions "one," "many," and "creativity" are the metaphysically ultimate notions, themselves "inexplicable either in terms of higher universals or in terms of the components participating in the concrescence" (PR 32), in terms of which the notion of a "thing," "being," or "entity" is rendered intelligible. Mathematician that he is, Whitehead is fully aware that a deductive system, be it mathematical or metaphysical, requires certain basic, ultimate concepts which are primitives, which are undefined, but whose mutual relationships are precisely defined and generate the contents of the system. The three notions constituting the Category of the Ultimate are such ultimate principles: "The sole appeal is to intuition" (PR 32). These three notions firmly ground on-goingness in the very foundation of

Whitehead's system, so that horizontal incoherence is no threat to the philosophy of organism. At the same time they in no way constitute a covert regression to monism, since the fully actual entities of the system are the individual occasions that emerge with each pulsation of the rhythmic flux between "many" and "one." Each individual among the "many" and each "one" that emerges are all alike actual occasions, while "creativity" is only the "universal of universals characterizing ultimate matter of fact" (PR 31), the ultimate principle descriptive of the nature of things, descriptive of that which is really real. Creativity transcends each individual actual occasion without being itself a higher order actuality, since it is simply the ultimate principle descriptive of the one-many relationship inhering in the coming-to-be of actual entities. Leclerc has written (p. 88) that "the actual entities must not be conceived as individually wholly independent and separate, merely superseding each other. Each is a creature of the creativity which proceeds perpetually to new creations." It is now clear that there is a perpetual advance to fresh actual occasions precisely because the actual entities are not wholly independent, but are rather linked in the creative process resulting from the one-many relationship that binds them together.

This point about the perpetual advance can be put in another way, a way that sheds still further light on Whitehead's system and corrects what I feel to be an overemphasis in Leclerc's book. Leclerc (p. 81) has quite rightly distinguished two senses of "process" in Whitehead's philosophy. Process is the fundamental feature of that which is really real and in its primary sense process is the coming-to-be of the individual actualities. But, as Leclerc notes (p. 81), "there is 'process' also in the derivative sense of the supersession of the epochal acts of becoming." Whitehead's technical terms for the first species of process are "microscopic process" and "concrescence"; the second species is referred to as "macroscopic process" and "transition."

Having made this distinction Leclerc remarks (p. 81): "Since the microscopic process is the fundamental metaphysical feature of actuality, we must, in examining the nature of actuality as process, attend primarily to that species." Putting the emphasis just this way raises the specter of horizontal incoherence, since it tends to appear that process is basically wrapped up in each individual actuality in such a way that there is no reason in the first principles why there should be a perpetual advance to fresh actual occasions. Leclerc is correct in noting that there are two species of process, but he does not adequately show how these are species of *one* process. I shall now make explicit how Whitehead's treatment of the Category of the Ultimate implies *one* process with two distinguishable species, a doctrine which completely removes the threat of horizontal incoherence.

It has been shown above that creativity is both the principle of concrete togetherness and the principle of novelty. Whitehead expresses the essential unity of these principles by saying that "the 'production of novel togetherness' is the ultimate notion embodied in the term 'concrescence'" (PR 32). The point to emphasize here is that both things, i.e. production of togetherness and production of novelty, *happen simultaneously:* to produce togetherness is to produce novelty, and vice versa. "The ultimate metaphysical principle is the advance from disjunction to conjunction, creating a novel entity other than the entities given in disjunction" (PR 32). It is because creativity links in the same set of relationships the production of togetherness and the production of novelty that on-goingness is built into the philosophy of organism. It happens, however, that from time to time in the exposition of his system Whitehead wishes to call attention, for purposes of analysis, to one or the other aspect of creativity, for they can be separated in thought although not in fact. Thus when he wishes to emphasize that " 'creativity' introduces novelty into the content of the many, which are the universe disjunctively" (PR 31–32), he speaks of macroscopic process, of the "creative advance," and of the movement from faded actual occasions to fresh actual occasions. "The macroscopic process is the transition from attained actuality to actuality in attainment" (PR 326). On the other hand, when he wishes to emphasize the coming together of the disjunctively diverse universe and the mutual accommodation of these diversities as they merge into one harmonious togetherness, he speaks of microscopic process, of the origin and mode of growth of the emerging actual occasion: "the microscopic process is the conversion of conditions which are merely real into determinate actuality" (PR 326). Macroscopic process emphasizes transition; microscopic process emphasizes growth. "The former process effects the transition from the 'actual' to the 'merely real'; and the latter process effects the growth from the real to the actual" (PR 326–27). But ontologically speaking, transition and growth are faces of the same coin. In fact, then, for Whitehead microscopic and macroscopic process are equally fundamental as features of that which is really real, since at bottom they are inseparable, though distinguishable. Consequently horizontal incoherence is avoided, as ongoingness is built right into the ultimate category of the system, but in such a way that there is no threat of vertical incoherence because there is no suggestion that creativity is an entity or thing at all.

This section has been long, because it has been necessary to introduce fundamental terminology essential to an understanding of Whitehead. By borrowing heavily from Leclerc I have put this terminology in the context of the great tradition of philosophical inquiry. I have introduced the notion of coming-to-be termed "concrescence"; this is important because Chapter 3 is a detailed analysis of concrescence. Also, and of greatest significance, in refining Leclerc's account of creativity I have indicated how Whitehead rationalizes the Bergsonian doctrine of flux. Commenting on Whitehead and his system, Newton P. Stallknecht writes:

> He has carried the philosophy of creation toward a brilliant culmination by combining with the productive contingency of Bergson the independence of the finite individual. In Whitehead's hands the philosophy of creation clearly distinguishes itself from a temporalist monism of constant creation.[16]

In presenting Whitehead's doctrine of creativity I have specified the precise sense in which Whitehead preserves the productive contingency of Bergson while modifying the latter's doctrine of flux into an intelligible system. Whitehead writes that "we have transformed the phrase, 'all things flow,' into the alternative phrase, 'the flux of things'" (PR 317). It is this shift that Stallknecht acknowledges by stressing the independence of the finite individual, and it has been the aim of this section to analyze the categories in Whitehead's system which accomplish the shift. Whitehead writes phrases such as, "The creativity of the world is the throbbing emotion of the past hurling itself into a new transcendent fact" (AI 227), but the "hurling" is, in his scheme, capable of rational elucidation. This characteristic of Whitehead's system will be reflected in the theory of artistic creation derived from it, in Chapter 8.

16. Newton P. Stallknecht, *Studies in the Philosophy of Creation* (Princeton, Princeton University Press, 1934), p. 132.

II. Eternal Objects

The second formative element consists of the eternal objects. It is essential in approaching Whitehead's system to understand the role played by eternal objects in the concrescence of actual occasions, for eternal objects bestow concrete definiteness upon actual entities, making them what they are. In Chapter 6 it will be argued that works of art have the ontological status of Whiteheadian propositions. Whitehead's doctrine of propositions will be discussed in detail in Chapter 3, but since a proposition is an unusual cross between actual entities and eternal objects, it is necessary to grasp the theory of eternal objects before either Chapter 3 or the aesthetic theory of Chapter 6 can be understood. Also, the distinction, shortly to be made between eternal objects of the objective species and eternal objects of the subjective species is crucial to the discussion of aesthetic experience in Chapter 7, particularly to the analysis of beauty in section v of that chapter.

Eternal objects are "Pure Potentials for the Specific Determination of Fact, *or* Forms of Definiteness" (PR 32). "A colour is eternal. It haunts time like a spirit. It comes and it goes. But where it comes, it is the same colour. It neither survives nor does it live. It appears when it is wanted" (SMW 88).

Whitehead also writes: "Any entity whose conceptual recognition does not involve a necessary reference to any definite actual entities of the temporal world is called an 'eternal object'" (PR 70).

Each actual entity, each individualization of the creativity, is an activity, but to be an individual act it must assume some determinate form. This it does by creatively deciding which eternal objects it will allow and which it will not allow to ingress into its concrescence. Whereas the change involved in the coming-to-be of an actual occasion is one with its very being, eternal objects are *essentially* aloof from change in that it is of their essence to be eternal. But they are involved *in* change in the sense that the very process of becoming which is any given actual occasion is the process of specifically determining, via selected eternal objects, the fact which is that actual occasion. Whitehead remarks that in the philosophy of organism,

> the actualities constituting the process of the world are conceived as exemplifying the ingression (or 'participation') of other things which constitute the potentialities of definiteness for any actual existence. The things which are temporal arise by their participation in the things which are eternal. [PR 63]

Leclerc emphasizes the metaphysical importance of the notion of potentiality to the philosophy of organism:

> There cannot be anything 'novel', that is, different from what is already 'actual', unless there be 'entities' which are 'potential'. . . . The point is that, by the ontological principle, something 'novel' cannot come into existence 'out of nowhere'; it must be 'given' as an 'unrealized potentiality'. This 'unrealized potentiality' must be constituted by 'entities'; the word 'unrealized' simply underlines the contrast of 'potentiality' with 'actuality'. Thus the notion of 'novelty' can have no meaning unless there be entities which are *'pure potentials'*. These are the eternal objects.[17]

The very notion of a dynamic, pluralistic universe presupposes pure potentials. Whitehead insists:

> It is evident that 'givenness' and 'potentiality' are both meaningless apart from a multiplicity of potential entities. These potentialities are the 'eternal objects.'

17. *Whitehead's Metaphysics*, p. 97.

Apart from 'potentiality' and 'givenness,' there can be no nexus of actual things in process of supersession by novel actual things. The alternative is a static monistic universe, without unrealized potentialities; since 'potentiality' is then a meaningless term. [PR 72]

There are eternal objects of the objective species and eternal objects of the subjective species. An adumbration of Whitehead's theory of prehensions is required to make this distinction clear.

During its concrescence an actual entity brings together into concrete unity the disjunctively diverse elements in its universe. It appropriates each of these elements via a prehension. Each prehension is dipolar.

> every prehension has its public side and its private side. Its public side is constituted by the complex datum prehended; and its private side is constituted by the subjective form through which a private quality is imposed on the public datum. [PR 444]

Eternal objects can function in the concrescence of an actual occasion only by being an element at one end or the other of a prehension which is, metaphorically speaking, "reaching out" to include an element in the concrescence of that actual occasion. The crucial question is, can all eternal objects function indifferently now at the public, or external end of one prehension, now at the private, or internal end of another prehension? The answer is that they cannot.

> An eternal object of the objective species can only obtain ingression in the first mode [i.e. at the public end of a prehension], and never in the second mode [i.e. at the private end of a prehension]. . . . Its sole avocation is to be an agent in objectification. It can never be an element in the definiteness of a subjective

form. The solidarity of the world rests upon the incurable objectivity of this species of eternal objects.
[PR 445–46]

Whitehead goes on to say: "Eternal objects of the objective species are the mathematical platonic forms" (PR
446). Geometrical shapes and numerical relationships are
eternal objects of the objective species.

Eternal objects of the subjective species function in a
more complicated manner. In their primary character they
appear at the private end of a prehension. They are the
qualitative clothing given the bare quantitative data of
the public side of any prehension. They define the subjective form of feeling of any given actual occasion; they
determine how it feels its objective data. A member of the
subjective species "is an emotion, or an intensity, or an
adversion, or an aversion, or a pleasure, or a pain" (PR
446). He specifically refers to "redness" as "the definiteness of an emotion which is a subjective form in the experience of A" (PR 447). All the so-called secondary qualities are eternal objects of the subjective species, as are
pains, likes, dislikes, etc. But although in their primary
character eternal objects of the subjective species appear
at the private end of a prehension, they may be transmuted
into a characteristic of a datum objectified for a given
actual occasion, and as such they function objectively.
Concrete examples will now be offered to clarify these
relationships.

A boy and his father both observe the boy's stepmother
enter the room. Both are aware of the same geometric
pattern; the objective datum of their two prehensions is
identical. Herein lies "the solidarity of the world," for this
objective datum, insofar as it is the locus of eternal objects
of the objective species, is quite independent of their perception of it. But while the boy entertains this objective

datum via a subjective form composed of such eternal objects of the subjective species as distrust and jealousy, his father entertains this same objective datum via a subjective form composed of such eternal objects as desire and respect. The two prehensions are quite different, though their initial datum is the same.

A second example will illustrate the more complicated functioning of eternal objects of the subjective species. A murderer peers out the window of his prison cell at the street below where there is a mob intent on lynching him. Each individual man in that mob is prehending the door of the jail through a subjective form that exemplifies anger, an eternal object of the subjective species. Anger is contributing to the definiteness of feeling of every man in that mob. The mob is the datum for the murderer and he transmutes [18] this eternal object, i.e. anger, present in all the individuals, into a characteristic of the mob as objectified by him. He perceives an angry mob. The eternal object of the subjective species, anger, is now functioning objectively.[19] The mob is objectified for the murderer by means of a component in the subjective form of each of the members of that mob. The eternal object, anger, has switched from its primary character of subjectivity to its secondary character of objectivity. It is quite likely that the objective datum "angry mob" is clothed with the eternal object of the subjective species "terror" in the prehension of the murderer.

These examples have been "macrocosmic" examples; it should be emphasized that Whitehead maintains that this activity of prehension finds its primary exemplification

18. Transmutation is a technical term explained below, pp. 53–54.
19. See PR 446: "[The eternal object of the subjective species] can be a private element in a subjective form, and also an agent in the objectification. In this latter character it may come under the operation of the category of transmutation and become a characteristic of a nexus as objectified for a percipient."

in the preconscious, "microcosmic" realm of actual occasions.

All these relationships, particularly that of "objectification," will be considered in greater detail in Chapter 3. At the moment I only wish to advance some very general notions about the ways in which eternal objects contribute definiteness to actual occasions. It is important to note here that these "forms of definiteness" can be called into play in either of two modes and that these two modes are not equally available to all eternal objects; in particular, eternal objects of the objective species cannot constitute the subjective form of an actual occasion.[20]

I have described certain characteristics of the manner in which eternal objects enter, or ingress into, actual occasions. As fully ingressed into an actual occasion, eternal objects are bound together into the concrete actuality which is that occasion. As resident in the realm of possibility, however, eternal objects exist in abrupt isolation from one another and are not woven together into concrete patterns, as they are when they have ingressed into an actual occasion. And yet it is a well-known feature of Whitehead's system that eternal objects exhibit an internal relatedness among themselves. The characteristics of eternal objects considered as denizens of the realm of possibility require clarification if this apparent paradox is to be resolved. Whitehead writes:

20. A. H. Johnson, in his extremely comprehensive article, "Whitehead's Theory of Actual Entities," *Philosophy of Science*, 12 (1945), 281, makes the surprising error of generalizing Whitehead's conclusions concerning eternal objects of the subjective species—i.e. that they can appear in both modes—and concluding that *all* eternal objects can appear in both modes. The most casual reading of PR 445–46 will reveal the inadequacy of Johnson's analysis—for example, "the solidarity of the world rests upon the incurable objectivity of this species of eternal objects."

there is a general fact of systematic mutual relatedness which is inherent in the character of possibility.
The realm of eternal objects is properly described as a
'realm,' because each eternal object has its status in
this general systematic complex of mutual relatedness. [SMW 161]

Each eternal object has a relational essence in virtue of
which it is determinately related to all other eternal objects. These determinate relationships "are internal relations. I mean by this that these relationships are constitutive of A [i.e. of any eternal object] . . . The internal
relationships of A conjointly form its significance" (SMW
160).[21] It follows from this that if one eternal object is ingredient in any particular actual occasion α, the internal
relatedness of that eternal object with all other eternal
objects entails that *all* eternal objects are thereby involved,
in some degree of graded relevance, in that actual occasion. Since all actual occasions have at least one ingredient eternal object, all actual occasions synthesize in
themselves all eternal objects.

All eternal objects are involved in α, but only some are
included, i.e. are fully ingredient, in α. Any actual occasion
"is to be conceived as a limitation; and . . . this process
of limitation can be still further characterised as a grada-
tion" (SMW 162). Not all of the host of eternal objects
could possibly ingress fully in α—many eternal objects are
mutually incompatible—and the activity which is the becoming of α is the decision by α of how relevant each eternal
object will be to α. α *grades* the relevance to it of all eternal
objects. All eternal objects are indeterminate as regards

21. Following Whitehead's practice, capital letters will be used to refer
to eternal objects and the Greek letters α and β will be used to refer
to particular actual occasions.

their relationships to actual occasions; eternal objects are
only externally related to actual occasions. But each actual
occasion is internally related to all eternal objects and acquires its own definiteness only by specifying its relationship to each eternal object. This it does by limiting, or
grading, the entry of eternal objects into its concrescence.
The concrescence of an actual occasion α involves an
inclusion or exclusion of each eternal object as an element
in its aesthetic synthesis.[22] Eternal objects can be (1)
included in the aesthetic synthesis; (2) excluded from the
synthesis so that they are "merely ingredient in the occasion
in respect to the determinate *how* this relationship is an
unfulfilled alternative, not contributing any aesthetic value,
except as forming an element in the systematic substratum
of unfulfilled content" (SMW 163); or (3) treated somewhat between these two extremes, remaining unfulfilled but
attaining aesthetic relevance. But however it is treated,
every eternal object is relevant to each actual occasion in
virtue of the web of relationships constituted by the internal relations that hold among eternal objects.

In addition to its relational essence each eternal object
has an individual essence:

> the individual essence is merely the eternal object
> considered as adding its own unique contribution to
> each actual occasion. This unique contribution is iden-
> tical for all such occasions in respect to the fact that
> the [eternal] object in all modes of ingression is just
> its identical self. But it varies from one occasion to

22. By the word "aesthetic" in this context Whitehead means to emphasize that he is speaking of the actual occasion *formaliter*, i.e. as it is in
its own immediate experience. See PR 81. He writes (PR 427), "an
actual fact is a fact of aesthetic experience," and also (PR 426), "An
intense experience is an aesthetic fact . . ." "Aesthetic" is not being used
here in the narrow sense it will have in Part II, below.

another in respect to the differences of its modes of ingression. [SMW 159]

When the mode of ingression permitted eternal object "A" by actual occasion α is that of maximum inclusion of "A" in α, when the relevance of value of "A" for α is at its maximum, then α includes the individual essence of "A" in its aesthetic synthesis. On the other hand, when "A" is ingredient in some actual occasion β in the lowest grade of relevance of value, the individual essence of "A" is excluded from β.

It is in virtue of the individual essences of eternal objects that Whitehead can speak of the principle of the "*Isolation of Eternal Objects* in the realm of possibility" (SMW 165). He stipulates: "The eternal objects are isolated, because their relationships *as possibilities* are expressible without reference to their respective individual essences" (SMW 165).[23] This "depends on the fact that the relational essence of an eternal object is not unique to that object" (SMW 165). Relational essences are tied to the notion, in logic, of a variable. The relational essence of an eternal object makes a particular determination

> of the *how* of some definite relationship of a definite eternal object A to a definite finite number n of other eternal objects, *without* any determination of the other n objects, $X_1, X_2, \ldots X_n$, except that they have, each of them, the requisite status to play their respective parts in that multiple relationship. [SMW 165]

For example, each shade of every color has a definite "how" relationship to every four-sided plane figure. This definite

23. Italics mine. The qualification "as possibilities" is crucial, since "in contrast to the realm of possibility the inclusion of eternal objects within an actual occasion means that in respect to some of their possible relationships there is a togetherness of their individual essences. This realized togetherness is the achievement of an emergent value" (SMW 165).

"how" relationship is a component of the relational essence of each shade and each figure, and binds all the shades and all the figures together internally, but these possible relationships are expressible without reference to the individual essence of any particular shade of blue or to the individual essence of any particular right-angled parallelogram. The relational essence of turquoise blue vis-à-vis any four-sided plane figure is not unique to turquoise blue, but is the same as that of pea green and jet black; thus the individual essence of turquoise blue is quite aloof from the relational essence of turquoise blue.

The apparent paradoxes with which this discussion opened can now be easily resolved. The togetherness of eternal objects in the realm of possibility is a very different sort of togetherness from that of eternal objects ingredient in one particular actual occasion. When included within one concrete actual occasion, several different eternal objects exhibit a togetherness of their *individual* essences, which is the achievement of an emergent value. As together in the realm of possibility, eternal objects exhibit a togetherness of their relational essences only, which, while a real and significant relatedness, preserves the isolation of eternal objects in the realm of possibility, since here individual essences stand aloof from the relational togetherness. The concrescent activity, which is any given actual occasion in process of becoming, is, in one of its aspects, the series of decisions whereby the individual essences of some eternal objects are integrated into concrete togetherness, and the individual essences of other eternal objects are rejected as components of the concrete togetherness. The relational character of the realm of possibility ensures that each actual occasion makes such a decision concerning every eternal object.

III. GOD

God is the third formative element. For present purposes it will suffice to exhibit just those features of God which serve to bind actual occasions and eternal objects into one coherent system. The architectonic of Part I of this essay requires that the discussion of God be divided into two parts. This final section of Chapter 2 will emphasize the relationships holding between God and eternal objects as well as the mutual interdependence of the three formative elements. Chapter 3 deals with concrescence, and since concrescence initiates with the concrescing actual occasion acquiring its subjective aim as a result of prehending God, section I of Chapter 3 will emphasize the relationships holding between God and actual occasions. The two sections taken together present an account of the manner in which God, the (1) *non-temporal*, (2) *actual* entity, mediates between the (1) *non-temporal* eternal objects and the (2) *actual* occasions which become and perish. The discussion of God is of crucial importance as a setting for the theory of artistic creation presented in Chapter 8. Artistic creation has frequently been linked to the notion of a divine madness or divine inspiration; with an exact account of the nature and function of God available, Chapter 8 will be able to specify in a very precise way the relationship between God and artistic creation.

The concept of God emerges from the metaphysical demand for a unique actual entity which links the realms of actuality and potentiality, providing for actuality the definiteness without which no single actual occasion could exist, and for potentiality the relationship to actuality, to agency, without which the resulting violation of the ontological principle would make an incoherence of the notion of a "realm" of eternal objects. Whitehead's system has here reached a point where internally it requires a

First Principle to relate the realms of actuality and potentiality, thereby providing a metaphysical basis for the emergence of definiteness. As Whitehead notes, "nothing, within any limited type of experience, can give intelligence to shape our ideas of any entity at the base of all actual things, unless the general character of things requires that there be such an entity" (SMW 174). The following comments will discover the manner in which the "general character of things" requires that there be a God. Obviously, God cannot be an arbitrarily introduced *deus ex machina*, else the system itself lapses into incoherence. Whitehead argues that the exact opposite must be the case: "God is not to be treated as an exception to all metaphysical principles, invoked to save their collapse. He is their chief exemplification" (PR 521). The sense in which God is "their chief exemplification" will be made explicit in section 1 of Chapter 3.

At the very beginning of this essay the point was made that where there is no process there can be no existence, and apart from actual entities there is no process. But eternal objects constitute a Category of Existence (PR 32). Hence the system demands that this mode of existence obtain its link with actuality. Speaking of the scope of the ontological principle, Whitehead writes:

> Everything must be somewhere; and here 'somewhere' means 'some actual entity.' Accordingly the general potentiality of the universe must be somewhere; since it retains its proximate relevance to actual entities for which it is unrealized. This 'proximate relevance' reappears in subsequent concrescence as final causation regulative of the emergence of novelty. This 'somewhere' is the non-temporal actual entity. Thus 'proximate relevance' means 'relevance as in the primordial mind of God.['] [PR 73]

The system requires God in the first place simply to preserve the ontological principle.

But God plays a far more crucial role in the operation of eternal objects than this rather obvious relationship suggests by itself. A more basic question concerns how it is possible for unrealized, abstract forms to be relevant to emerging actual entities. Whitehead asks:

> In what sense can unrealized abstract form be relevant? What is its basis of relevance? 'Relevance' must express some real fact of togetherness among forms. The ontological principle can be expressed as: All real togetherness is togetherness in the formal constitution of an actuality. So if there be a relevance of what in the temporal world is unrealized, the relevance must express a fact of togetherness in the formal constitution of a non-temporal actuality. [PR 48]

For eternal objects to be relevant to creative process there is required a "real togetherness" of eternal objects, a web of general relationships among eternal objects, and this *real* togetherness must be a formal aspect of God. Whitehead makes this point more explicitly in another context: "The general relationships of eternal objects to each other, relationships of diversity and of pattern, are their relationships in God's conceptual realization. Apart from this realization, there is mere isolation indistinguishable from nonentity" (PR 392).

These quotations suggest strongly that God's primordial valuation of the realm of eternal objects is identical with the web of relationships constituted by the internal relatedness of eternal objects. The following comparisons substantiate this conclusion. It is a basic tenet of Whitehead's system that God links concrescing actualities with the realm of eternal objects; section II above makes the point that the web of internal relatedness entails that the eternal objects ingredient in an actual occasion, through their relationship to all other eternal objects, involve all eternal objects, in some degree of graded relevance, in that one concrescence. In the above passage Whitehead also holds that apart from God's conceptual realization there would be in the realm of eternal objects only "mere isolation indistinguishable from nonentity"; section II above makes the point that the "internal relationships of A conjointly form its significance," i.e. that they "are constitutive of A; for an entity which stands in internal relations has no being as an entity not in these relations" (SMW 160). The following passage summarizes Whitehead's doctrine of the primordial nature of God, and strengthens the claim that God's conceptual valuation is identical with the web of relationships constituted by the internal relatedness of eternal objects:

> The things which are temporal arise by their participation in the things which are eternal. The two sets are mediated by a thing which combines the actuality of what is temporal with the timelessness of what is potential. This final entity [God] is the divine element in the world, by which the barren inefficient disjunction of abstract potentialities obtains primordially the efficient conjunction of ideal realization. . . . By reason of the actuality of this primordial valuation of pure potentials, each eternal object has a definite, effective relevance to each concrescent process. Apart from such orderings, there would be a complete disjunction of eternal objects unrealized in the temporal world. Novelty would be meaningless, and inconceivable. [PR 63–64]

The conclusion emerges that the three formative elements are tightly interwoven into a mutual interdependence. The discussion of eternal objects, in analyzing their relational essences, was implicitly forced to assume

God's primordial vision. Again, the final sentences of the above passage make it clear that the dynamic surge of the creativity into novel concrescence presupposes not simply a realm of possibility but also the primordial valuation of pure potentials which generates the relevance of each pure potential to each instance of concrescent process. But it should not be inferred that God creates eternal objects in his primordial valuation; here also there is mutual interdependence. Whitehead writes that God "does not create eternal objects; for his nature requires them in the same degree that they require him. This is an exemplification of the coherence of the categoreal types of existence" (PR 392). As has been shown, apart from God's primordial existence eternal objects are "indistinguishable from nonentity." But it is also true that without eternal objects God's primordial existence is impossible: "Eternal objects are inseparable from God's primordial existence; they are the primordial 'definiteness' apart from which no existence or creativity, even in the primordial instance of God, is possible at all." [24] Actuality, even the primordial instance of actuality which is God, presupposes definiteness; hence creativity also presupposes eternal objects even in its primordial, aboriginal instance. A more precise sense in which creativity presupposes God will emerge in section 1 of Chapter 3.

It takes pistons, a sparking device, and some fuel to result in an operating, pulsing, dynamic engine. If any of these three be lacking, there is no dynamic system. Remove the sparking device or the fuel and you still have pistons, but pistons resting inert in their casings are lifeless and pointless when compared to the vibrating, thrusting pistons of a dynamic system. Likewise, eternal objects in the "isolation indistinguishable from nonentity" are inert, lifeless, and ungraded in relevance when compared to eternal

24. Leclerc, *Whitehead's Metaphysics*, pp. 199–200.

objects linked by the web of relational essences which is God's primordial vision.

It is instructive to compare Whitehead's system with Plato's *Timaeus*. Cornford's interpretation of the *Timaeus* is as follows:

> both the Demiurge and chaos are symbols: neither is to be taken quite literally, yet both stand for real elements in the world as it exists. . . . [For example, since chaos] never existed before [the] cosmos, [it] must stand for some element that is now and always present in the working of the universe.[25]

Whitehead's three formative elements have this same role to play in his philosophy. It is pointless to ask if God created eternal objects; not only are both nontemporal, so that to imply that one is "prior" to the other is meaningless, but the very asking of this question is to miss the point of the role played by the formative elements in Whitehead's system. Each formative element stands for some element that is now and always present in the working of a world without beginning or end. The three formative elements in their interaction are mutually interdependent; from their mutual interaction emerges the universe of actual occasions. The next chapter will describe this emergence, and some further facets of the interaction that produces it, by considering in detail the process of concrescence, the coming-to-be, which is common to all actual occasions. It will begin by completing the study of the formative element, God, through a consideration of how concrescence initiates with the concrescing actual occasion acquiring a subjective aim from its prehension of God.

25. Francis M. Cornford, *Plato's Cosmology* (London, Routledge and Kegan Paul, 1937), p. 37; see also p. 176.

3. Concrescence

CHAPTER 2 only briefly described the central characteristics of each of the formative elements. This chapter will uncover the generic characteristics of the process, called "concrescence," which is the result of the mutual interaction of these formative elements and from which emerges the concrete actual entity. Certain aspects of the formative elements, aspects merely adumbrated earlier, will here acquire more clarity. The analysis of concrescence will also introduce and systematically explain several concepts which will be used extensively in the aesthetic theory of Part II; in particular, the concepts "proposition," "subjective aim," "transmutation," and "reversion."

At the conclusion of the last chapter God was related to eternal objects; he will now be related to actual occasions by showing how, as final cause, he initiates the concrescence of each and every actual occasion via subjective aims.

1. ORIGIN OF SUBJECTIVE AIMS

To be a mature actual occasion is to be fully definite. There are then no more decisions regarding possible forms of definiteness to make—they have all been made. So in a very basic sense all actual occasions are dependent upon God, for without God the forms of definiteness would be indistinguishable from nonentity and decisions productive of concreteness would be impossible. But there is a more specific manner in which all actual occasions can be said to depend on God; in a limited sense of the word "create," God can be said to "create" all actual occasions.

In an important passage Whitehead writes, "God is the aboriginal instance of this creativity, and is therefore the aboriginal condition which qualifies its action. It is the function of actuality to characterize the creativity, and God is the eternal primordial character" (PR 344). In these sentences Whitehead is saying more than that God merely conditions creativity by being an instance of creativity. Leclerc describes the uniqueness of status given to God in the above passage:

> By the phrase 'God is the aboriginal condition which qualifies the action of creativity', Whitehead means that in addition to each ordinary actual entity 'conditioning' creativity, God also 'conditions' creativity in every instance of its individualization. This God does through his basic metaphysical role of providing the subjective aim for every actual entity.[1]

Whitehead is *not* saying, then, that

> God is in the past of all other actualities, in the sense that God was once the solely existing actual entity. A consistent metaphysical pluralism cannot hold that creativity originally had only a single instantiation. Moreover, such a conception of God would constitute a violation of all the categories of Whitehead's system.[2]

Whitehead *is* insisting that God has a crucial role in the birth of every actual occasion. By playing this role, God does in a very real sense "create" each actual occasion, though Whitehead warns us that the phrase "God as creator" is "apt to be misleading by its suggestion that the ultimate creativity of the universe is to be ascribed to God's

1. *Whitehead's Metaphysics*, p. 195.
2. Ibid., pp. 194–95.

volition" (PR 343–44). As was emphasized in Chapter 2, each actual occasion is a process of self-creation—creativity, not God, is the metaphysical ultimate for Whitehead—but the sense in which God is creator must now be explored.

In a brief discussion of prehensions in Chapter 2 [3] the point was made that an actual occasion "reaches out" to include the elements of its universe in its own concrescence; it "grasps," "takes account of," or "absorbs" by means of "prehensions" the disjunctive diversity of elements which it unites into its concrete unity. Prehensions are, respectively, either physical or conceptual as they grasp either another actual occasion or an eternal object. A third type of prehension, a hybrid physical prehension, occurs when a concrescing actual occasion "objectifies" a datum actual occasion by seizing on one of the conceptual prehensions, or conceptual feelings, of that datum actual occasion and objectifying that actual occasion as it is represented by that particular conceptual feeling. One actual entity objectified by every actual occasion at its inception is God, and God is objectified by means of a hybrid physical feeling. [4]

In God's primordial conceptual vision are included all the possibilities relevant to the concrescence of every actual occasion. These possibilities are groupings of eternal objects made relevant to each concrescence by God's primordial prehension of the network of relationships holding among them; it is by reason of God's vision that the *abstract* relevance of eternal objects becomes *selectively* relevant to particular actual occasions. Any given actual occasion is conditioned by the limitations laid upon it by the demands of its universe. Given these limitations, there remains, how-

3. See above, p. 27.
4. Whitehead uses the terms "prehension" and "feeling" interchangeably when he intends by the former term to refer to a positive prehension. "Feeling" best seems to sum up the relationship I have suggested by the phrases "grasp," "become aware of," and "absorb." The sense of the term "feeling," or "prehension" will emerge more clearly in what follows.

ever, an area of indeterminacy within which that occasion faces alternatives awaiting its decision. In its hybrid physical prehension of God, this actual occasion prehends not God in his full concreteness as an actual entity [5] but God as objectified by those conceptual prehensions of eternal objects which constitute relevant alternatives capable of leading to the satisfaction of that particular actual occasion conditioned by its particular antecedent circumstances.

God is not neutral in his preference as to which of the relevant possibilities be selected by the concrescing actual occasion as its subjective aim. But neither can God coerce the actual occasion into realizing one among the alternatives. God "lures" the actual occasion toward that realization which will result in the achievement of maximum value in the world. "God's immanence in the world in respect to his primordial nature is an urge towards the future based upon an appetite in the present" (PR 47). To say in Whitehead's technical language that God has an appetite generating an urge toward the future is merely to say that he "feels" the present "physically," "conceptually" envisions the greatest intensity of value toward which that present can lead, and has an urge to have that possibility actualized in the future. For example, thirst is an appetite or urge, arising from the physical feeling of dryness combined with the conceptual feeling of slaking that dryness; were the conceptual element lacking there would be no thirst, merely a dull ache here-now. God's "urging" toward the realization of intensity of value constitutes, then, a lure. Where this lure is successful the actual occasion in question realizes in its satisfaction the relevant possibility leading to the greatest intensity of value.

5. As in any prehension, the "object" is prehended under a perspective. In Whitehead's terminology this means that one of its feelings (a conceptual feeling in this case) is selected to objectify that object for that percipient. See PR 361.

God is the principle of concretion; namely, he is that
actual entity from which each temporal concrescence
receives that initial aim from which its self-causation
starts. That aim determines the initial gradations of
relevance of eternal objects for conceptual feeling; and
constitutes the autonomous subject in its primary
phase of feelings with its initial conceptual valuations,
and with its initial physical purposes. [PR 374]

Whitehead writes:

the initial stage of the aim is rooted in the nature
of God, and its completion depends on the self-causation of the subject-superject [PR 373]. . . . [Each
temporal entity] derives from God its basic conceptual
aim, relevant to its actual world, yet with indetermina-
tions awaiting its own decisions. This subjective aim,
in its successive modifications, remains the unifying
factor governing the successive phases of interplay between physical and conceptual feelings. [PR 343]

Each actual occasion has a certain amount of elbow room in
its development. It may modify its initial vision of itself
derived from God and thereby fail to realize the full intensity of value present in God's appetition. This is the
freedom in the universe. It may also be the case that events
have reached an impasse where the most desirable alternative is bad: "if the best be bad, then the ruthlessness of God
can be personified as Atè, the goddess of mischief. The
chaff is burnt" (PR 373).

It is God's primordial conceptual valuation of eternal
objects which constitutes the relevance for the concrescing
actual occasion, via a hybrid physical feeling of God, of the
realm of possibility. This is the formal aspect of novelty
in the world. In deriving its subjective aim, i.e. the goal
toward which it will direct its process of self-realization,

the concrescing actual occasion couples the concreteness of the limitations impinging on it from its past with the abstractness of that particular relevant possibility revealed by the primordial vision of God which it has decided to actualize in its becoming. Such a coupling of the concrete and the abstract, Whitehead terms a proposition. Hence, Whitehead's formal definition of subjective aim: "The 'subjective aim,' which controls the becoming of a subject, is that subject feeling a proposition with the subjective form of purpose to realize it in that process of self-creation" (PR 37).

In summary, the subjective aim of any given actual occasion is derived from God and constitutes the goal toward which that entity directs its self-creative process. The attaining of the goal constitutes the satisfaction of that actual occasion. The remainder of this chapter will analyze the component phases by which an actual occasion progresses from its selection of a subjective aim to its satisfaction.

II. Phase I of Concrescence

In its initial phase the concrescing actual occasion already possesses, in a sense, a unity, an indivisible togetherness, as a result of its subjective aim. But this unity provided by the subjective aim is an ideal unity, not a concrete unity of feeling. In this initial phase the actual occasion is composed of many unintegrated prehensions. It will be recalled that each actual occasion unites into a concrete unity all of the already constituted actual entities, some eternal objects, and God. In the initial phase of its concrescence, an actual occasion is merely the sum of all its separate prehensions of this multitude of objects. The process which is the concrescence is the process of fusing into a *unity* what is initially merely a *sum* of prehensions.

The process of concrescence is divisible into an initial
stage of many feelings, and a succession of subsequent
phases of more complex feelings integrating the earlier
simpler feelings, up to the satisfaction which is one
complex unity of feeling. This is the 'genetic' analysis
of the satisfaction. [PR 337]

It might be helpful to visualize this situation in terms of a
triangle. The base of the triangle constitutes the unintegrated prehensions of the sum of the other actual entities
and eternal objects. Then, via higher phases of integration,
more complicated prehensions arise which integrate groups
of simpler prehensions so that the triangle steadily narrows
until that one complex prehension, or unity of feeling, is
reached which is the apex of the triangle, i.e. the satisfaction
of the concrescing actual occasion. The purpose of this
chapter is to discover, examine, and clarify the characteristics of these phases of concrescence.

The first phase of concrescence is variously labeled by
Whitehead the primary phase, the initial phase, the receptive phase, or the conformal phase. The initial phase is
composed entirely of physical feelings. In this stage are
lined up "side by side" the multitude of prehensions of the
actual occasions which compose the actual world of that
concrescing subject. Included among these physical feelings is the hybrid physical feeling of God, described above.
These initial physical feelings, the hybrid physical feeling
of God included, are all simple physical feelings, i.e. they
each have as a datum only one actual occasion (PR 361).

Given any simple physical prehension within the conformal phase, we can distinguish two subphases, the datum
and the subjective response (PR 179). The datum constitutes the public side of a prehension and the subjective
response constitutes the private side of a prehension; this

distinction has already been made in connection with the discussion in Chapter 2 of the objective and subjective species of eternal objects.[6] The initial datum is one single actual occasion in the past of the subject actual occasion. This past, or object, actual occasion is itself the amalgamation of many prehensions. The present, or subject, actual occasion selects one of the prehensions of the past actual occasion it is objectifying to stand forth as the general representative of that past actual occasion; the selected prehension is then said to objectify that past actual occasion for the present subject occasion. The past actual occasion has been reduced to a "perspective" constituted by one of its own feelings (PR 361). The subjective response has consisted of the decision by the subject as to which feeling of the past actual occasion will be selected to objectify that past actual occasion. It is crucial for an understanding of this subjective response to recognize that each separate prehension does not choose the perspective of its initial datum independently of all the other prehensions which in aggregate compose the subject actual occasion at that phase of its concrescence. Quite to the contrary, it is a Categoreal Obligation, that of subjective unity, that: "The many feelings which belong to an incomplete phase in the process of an actual entity, though unintegrated by reason of the incompleteness of the phase, are compatible for integration by reason of the unity of their subject" (PR 39). When deciding upon a perspective, a feeling is guided by the subjective aim of the subject and the manner in which its fellow feelings are contributing to that aim. It is as though just enough basketballs were simultaneously thrown into a baby's playpen to cover the bottom; for a moment there would be a piling up of balls, but the "aim" of gravity would quickly encourage them to settle out, mutually making way for one another until the

6. See above, p. 27.

pen were smoothly covered. Just so, the aim at the satisfaction (a telic, not a mechanical cause, however) encourages the prehensions to "cover" the actual world in a mutually consistent manner. In this process of adjustment, negative prehensions serve to eliminate, or reject for inclusion, incompatible elements. A negative prehension "holds its datum as inoperative in the progressive concrescence of prehensions constituting the unity of the subject" (PR 35), but its subjective form retains importance. A negative prehension "expresses a bond"; through *its* subjective form it "adds to the emotional complex" which is the subjective form of the final, "satisfied" subject (PR 66). For all prehensions, then, positive and negative, "the determinations of successive phases of subjective forms, whereby the integrations have the characters that they do have, depends [depend] on the unity of the subject imposing a mutual sensitivity upon the prehensions" (PR 359).

In summary, the first phase of concrescence achieves, via eliminations, a multitude of compatible perspectives of all entities in the actual universe of the concrescing subject. Included among these perspectives is the hybrid physical prehension of God whereby the possibilities for novelty relevant to that unique subject have been made available as a lure toward the realization of greater intensities of value, and have been integrated by the subject into a subjective aim which conditions the mutual sensitivity of the host of simple physical prehensions.

III. PHASE II OF CONCRESCENCE

The second phase of concrescence is quite simple. Phases two, three, and four are all considered by Whitehead as supplementary phases, or originative phases, or integrative phases. The labels indicate that, as opposed to the initial, conformal, or receptive phase, these three higher phases are the great sources of novelty. The second phase, the first of the three higher phases, is the conceptual stage, or the stage of conceptual feelings.

Conceptual feelings are derived from physical feelings. It is again a Categoreal Obligation that: "From each physical feeling there is the derivation of a purely conceptual feeling whose datum is the eternal object determinant of the definiteness of the actual entity, or of the nexus, physically felt" (PR 39–40). Eternal objects are involved in both physical feelings and conceptual feelings, but with a difference. In a physical feeling an eternal object is felt as immanent, i.e. as a realized determinant of concreteness. In a conceptual feeling an eternal object is felt as transcendent, i.e. as a general *capacity* for determination (PR 366–67). What happens in the second phase of concrescence is that the eternal objects, bedded fast in the concreteness of exclusive determination of a particular actual entity in the conformal phase, are pried loose, or abstracted from, that determinateness and become, as objects for the conceptual feeling, transcendent. The difference can be expressed this way; whereas the datum of a physical feeling is an actual occasion, the datum of a conceptual feeling is an eternal object, a pure potential. From a regular physical prehension arises a conceptual feeling of an eternal object already realized in the temporal world. From the hybrid physical prehension of God may arise a conceptual feeling of a novel eternal object: "The light that never was, on sea or land" (AI 270).[7] Only God can conjure up conceptual feelings that do not depend on prior physical feelings. "Unfettered conceptual valuation, 'infinite' in Spinoza's sense of that term, is only possible once in the universe; since that creative act is objectively immortal as an inescapable condition characterizing creative action" (PR 378).

With the presence of conceptual feelings the actual

7. This eternal object is, of course, novel only in the sense that it has never before been prehended by a *temporal* actual occasion.

occasion has acquired a mental pole over against its physical pole. "The mental pole originates as the conceptual
counterpart of operations in the physical pole. The two
poles are inseparable in their origination. The mental pole
starts with the conceptual registration of the physical pole"
(PR 379). The distinctive importance of these initial conceptual feelings of the mental pole centers about their
character as valuations. The physical feelings of the conformal phase are compatible for integration. Since all
incompatibilities have been eliminated, the higher phases
cannot effect consolidation of the physical feelings by
means of negative prehensions (PR 368). The consolidation and integration of later stages is accomplished in part
by valuation. Valuation constitutes the subjective form of
conceptual feelings (PR 367). The data of conceptual
feelings are transcendent eternal objects; their subjective
forms are either "valuation up" or "valuation down," adversion or aversion. The subjective form of any conceptual
feeling is not independent of the subjective forms of the
other conceptual feelings; *all* subjective forms are subordinate to the subjective aim of the concrescing subject.
The example of the settling basketballs, applied above to
physical prehensions and negative prehensions, is therefore
equally appropriate to conceptual prehensions and valuations. As a result of valuation, the importance of a given
datum eternal object for the final unity of feeling which is
the satisfaction is either enhanced or attenuated.

Conceptual Reversion

Within this second phase, that of conceptual feelings,
two extremely important operations occur; conceptual reversion and transmutation. Reverted feelings, like ordinary
conceptual feelings, are derived from a physical feeling, but
what makes the difference is that the physical feeling involved in the case of reverted conceptual feelings is the

hybrid physical feeling of God. The conceptual feelings
resulting from conceptual reversion are dependent upon
the conceptual feelings derived from ordinary simple physical feelings in that their data are "partially identical with,
and partially diverse from, the eternal objects forming the
data" for a regular conceptual feeling (PR 380). That is,
the content of a reverted conceptual feeling has some
eternal objects in common with those immanent in certain prior physical feelings, but in prying these eternal
objects loose from the immanent status they have in these
physical feelings, it introduces relevant novelty of content.
These "proximate" novelties are then conceptually felt in
the reverted conceptual feeling. "This is the process by
which the subsequent enrichment of subjective forms, both
in qualitative pattern, and in intensity through contrast,
is made possible by the positive conceptual prehension of
relevant alternatives" (PR 381). A specific example of what
Whitehead has in mind here is furnished by Hume's well-
known discussion of the missing shade of blue: [8] even
though one has never seen a particular shade of blue, one
can, given other shades of blue, conceptually supply the
missing shade. This is not a trivial and insignificant exception to the sensationalist principle upon which Hume erects
his philosophy, Whitehead maintains, but a ubiquitous
factor in all concrescence. Upon deeper analysis, "Hume's
principle of the derivation of conceptual experience from
physical experience remains without any exception," for
the reverted conceptual feeling in a temporal occasion is
derived from its "hybrid physical feeling of the relevancies
conceptually ordered in God's experience" (PR 382).[9]

8. The discussion is found in the first section of the *Treatise* and is
quoted by Whitehead at PR 132–33.

9. Properly, Whitehead should have excepted God from this complete
generalization of Hume's principle. I have already noted Whitehead's
statement that "Unfettered conceptual valuation . . . is only possible
once in the universe" (above, p. 50). But that once, the primordial

Reversion is the source of novelty, but "reversion is always limited by the necessary inclusion of elements identical with elements in feelings of the antecedent phase" (PR 381).

Transmutation

As a result of the initial or conformal phase, an actual occasion is a conglomeration of physical feelings compatible for integration into the final feeling which is the satisfaction of the concrescing subject. Conceptual feelings have merely aggravated the situation by multiplying the feelings that must be integrated, though it has been indicated that valuation, the subjective form of conceptual feelings (reversions included), can, in effect, eliminate from feeling by attenuating the importance for the final satisfaction of a given datum eternal object. There is initially a conglomeration of atomic, or microcosmic, entities, and they have to be integrated in such a way as to account for macrocosmic perception, for everyday perception of rocks, trees, people, etc. As Whitehead notes, this is "a perplexity which is inherent in all monadic cosmologies. Leibniz in his *Monodology* meets the same difficulty by a theory of 'confused' perception. But he fails to make clear how 'confusion' originates" (PR 40). This whole account of integration can be viewed as an attempt to give a reasoned account of the Leibnizian doctrine of "confusion." At this point the Whiteheadian account introduces an effective categoreal condition for integrating a conglomeration of feelings, viz. transmutation, which also accomplishes the shift from the microcosmic to the macrocosmic.

Transmutation is a simple operation. A collection of entities, or a nexus, most members of which exhibit a cer-

---

vision of God, is "an inescapable condition characterizing creative action." Hume's principle *does* hold, however, for all temporal actual occasions.

tain quality, is transmuted into a single datum exhibiting
that common quality. An example will help. The many
actual occasions which constitute a nexus are, say, characterized by the eternal object "red," i.e. they feel "redly."
A subsequent, subject actual occasion, as it begins its concrescence, prehends each of the actual occasions in the
nexus. It therefore exhibits a conglomeration of simple
physical feelings, corresponding to the collection of actual
occasions in the nexus. Most of these simple physical feelings consequently have the eternal object "red" as datum.
There 'arises in the conceptual phase of that concrescing
subject one conceptual feeling with that eternal object
"red" as datum. The important point is that this "conceptual feeling has an impartial relevance to the above-
mentioned various simple physical feelings of the various
members of the nexus" (PR 383). The emergence of this
conceptual feeling constitutes the first stage of transmutation. Transmutation is completed in a yet higher phase of
concrescence, the second supplemental phase which is the
phase of simple comparative feelings. Because of the impartial relevance of this conceptual feeling to the majority
of simple physical feelings by means of which the subject
occasion prehends the external nexus, at the higher stage
of simple comparative feelings this conceptual feeling and
all the involved simple physical feelings are integrated into
one transmuted physical feeling which feels the entire external nexus as one entity qualified by the datum of the
conceptual feeling involved, i.e. by the eternal object "red."
It should be noted that one single prehension has emerged
where there were initially many. Transmutation thus provides an explanation of how the number of unintegrated
prehensions decreases in the course of concrescence. The
machinery involved in the second stage of transmutation
has not, however, been fully described; a careful analysis of
the phase of simple comparative feelings is required.

IV. PHASE III OF CONCRESCENCE

In the first phase of concrescence simple physical feelings emerge. In the second phase each simple physical feeling gives rise to a conceptual feeling. Now, in the third phase of simple comparative feelings, each simple physical feeling is integrated with its conceptual counterpart.

> The integration of each simple physical feeling with its conceptual counterpart produces in a subsequent phase [the phase of simple comparative feelings] a physical feeling whose subjective form of re-enaction has gained or lost subjective intensity according to the valuation up, or the valuation down, in the conceptual feeling. So far there is merely subjective re-adjustment of the subjective forms. This is the phase of physical purpose. The effect of the conceptual feeling is thus, so far, merely to provide that the modified subjective form is not merely derived from the re-enaction of the objectified actual entity. [PR 380]

Involved in this integration is the notion of a contrast. Contrasts are "Modes of Synthesis of Entities in one Prehension" (PR 33). Category of Explanation xvii begins: "That whatever is a datum for a feeling has a unity *as felt*. Thus the many components of a complex datum have a unity: this unity is a 'contrast' of entities" (PR 36).

Figure 1 consolidates the material presented to this point and prepares for the advance to the final phase of conscious feelings. The circle *a* represents the simple physical feeling which is the objectification for the concrescing subject of the datum actual occasion. The line *x* indicates the advance to the conceptual feeling *b* derived from *a*. The circle *b'* represents a second order conceptual feeling, i.e. a reverted feeling, which may or may not arise. Circle *c* represents the simple comparative feeling which arises by comparing,

or holding in contrast, *a* and *b*. The bracket *y* indicates
the contrast between *a* and *b* which is the datum for *c*.
Since *b* is a pure potential and *a* is an objectified actual
entity, the contrast between *a* and *b* satisfies the definition,

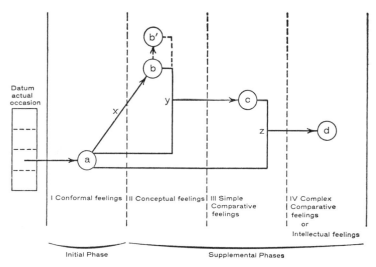

Figure 1. Phases of Concrescence

to be given immediately, of a proposition. As the datum
for *c*, *y* is a proposition; the comparative feeling *c* can hence
be called a propositional feeling.

> A proposition is [a] new kind of entity. It is a hybrid
> between pure potentialities and actualities. . . . [It]
> is the potentiality of an actual world including a def-
> inite set of actual entities in a nexus of reactions in-
> volving the hypothetical ingression of a definite set of
> eternal objects. [PR 282]

The definite actual entities involved are termed the
"logical subjects" of the proposition, and the eternal object involved, simple or complex, is termed the "predicative

pattern" of the proposition. A proposition is a lure for feeling. The simple comparative feeling c arises in response to the lure which is y. The simple comparative feeling c is more properly termed a propositional feeling when it belongs to the concrescence of a sophisticated actual entity productive of intellectual feelings at phase IV. If the subject actual occasion in the process of concrescence is of a primitive type, its prehensions do not proceed to integrations more sophisticated than c. Such primitive actual occasions produce a comparative feeling at c that is more aptly called a "physical purpose" than a "propositional feeling." If c is a physical purpose, the eternal object pried out of its immanence at a into transcendence at b just sinks back at c into integration with itself as immanent and the contrast between potentiality and actuality vaporizes. Hence the inappropriateness of the label "propositional feeling." In this case of a physical purpose, a and c cannot, however, be regarded as identical. Since the subjective form of b has, as previously explained, valuated the eternal object involved either up or down, c represents a physical feeling whose subjective form of re-enaction may have gained or lost subjective intensity as a result of the valuation at b. Consequently, c may have its efficacy in the final satisfaction either enhanced or attenuated.

Before proceeding to a discussion of the fourth phase of concrescence, represented by the circle d, an enlargement of the initial portion of Figure 1, presented as Figure 2, will be used to clarify transmutation.

Given a cluster of datum actual occasions at the left of Figure 2, most of which are characterized by the same eternal object, "red," a series of simple physical feelings occurs on the same vertical plane as a, labeled a_1, a_2, etc. These physical feelings a, a_1, and a_2, etc. objectify their datum from a perspective including red. The circle b here represents the emergence of a single conceptual feeling with the eternal object "red" appearing transcendently as datum. The conceptual feeling b has impartial relevance to the whole series of a's (PR 383, 384–86); hence the simple comparative feeling c which emerges at the third phase, be

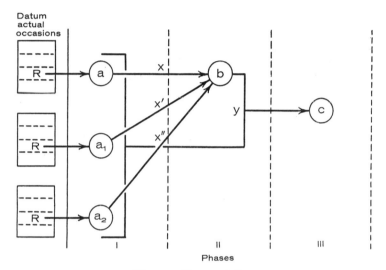

Figure 2. Transmutation

it a physical purpose or a propositional feeling, contrasts (as indicated by bracket y) b with the involved physical feelings. This particular simple comparative feeling c is called a transmuted physical feeling, since it prehends the entire external nexus as one entity qualified by the eternal object "red." The valuation at b of the eternal object involved determines, of course, the efficacy of the transmuted physical feeling in the final satisfaction of the concrescing subject.

It might be well to emphasize again the role transmutation is designed to play in concrescence. Whitehead writes:

it must be noted that the integration of simple physical feelings into a complex physical feeling only provides for the various actual entities of the nexus being felt as separate entities requiring each other. We have to account for the substitution of the one nexus in place of its component actual entities. [PR 384]

The one emergent conceptual feeling with *impartial relevance* to the various actual entities of the nexus is the key to the emergence of *one* nexus rather than a mere tight togetherness of many separate entities felt as "requiring each other." The movement from "many" to "one" required, as Leibniz saw, by any monadic cosmology, is accomplished via the emergence of an impartially relevant conceptual feeling in transmutation. One transmuted physical feeling supersedes a host of simple physical feelings of a host of actual entities, and as a result the host of microcosmic existences is replaced for that concrescing subject by the one macrocosmic existent which is the nexus emergent in transmutation. The category of transmutation provides "a physical feeling of a nexus as one entity with its own categoreal type of existence" (PR 384). By means of transmutation, rocks, trees, people, etc. emerge as distinct entities from the welter of multitudinous microcosmic actual occasions. But these entities which emerge as a result of transmutation are abstractions from the full concreteness of their component actual occasions; to treat these derivative entities as metaphysically ultimate is to commit the Fallacy of Misplaced Concreteness (SMW 52).

One further characteristic of transmutation must be emphasized; it effects the transfer from the conceptual realm to the physical realm of what emerges conceptually as a novelty. Transmutation

> governs the transition from conceptual feelings in one actual entity to physical feelings either in a supervening phase of itself or in a later actual entity. What is conceptual earlier is felt physically later in an extended

rôle. Thus, for instance, a new 'form' has its emergent
ingression conceptually by reversion, and receives de-
layed exemplification physically . . . [PR 387–88]

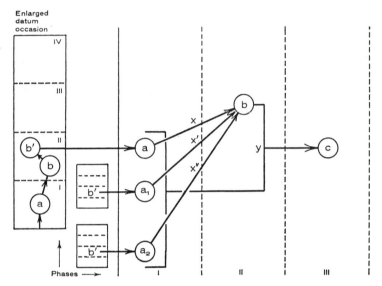

Figure 3. Reversion in Datum

The two ways in which this transfer can occur are illustrated
in Figures 3 and 4. In both these diagrams the situation is
essentially that of Figure 2; *c* is a transmuted physical feeling. The datum actual occasion has been sketched in additional detail so that in Figure 3 it is clear that novelty
emerges through the reverted conceptual feelings, *b'*, *in the
data*, while in Figure 4 it is clear that the locus of the reversion, *b'*, is the subject actual entity. Whitehead also
admits the possibility of a double reversion (PR 386); this
could be illustrated easily by including both reversions in
one diagram, i.e. by putting the left side of Figure 3 together with the right side of Figure 4.

In Figure 3 the vast majority of actual occasions in the

datum nexus are objectified by the reverted conceptual feeling *b′*. Consider the example, given in Chapter 2, of the murderer looking down out of his cell window at the angry

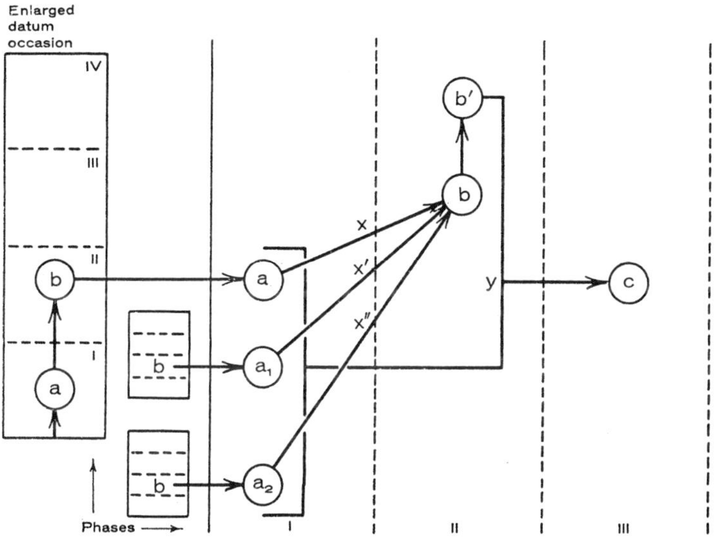

Figure 4. Reversion in Subject

mob below. Anger is a reverted conceptual feeling which is a novelty in each member of the crowd. The crowd emerges as a nexus, as a distinct entity, because "anger" has impartial relevance to the members of the nexus and by means of transmutation the one nexus is substituted for the component members of the crowd in the perception of the murderer. Whitehead's point in stressing the movement from conceptual status to physical status is that although anger arises conceptually in the individual members of the mob, for the murderer anger is nobody's dream: it is a real physical fact in the physical world. To make this clearer, I will introduce a double reversion. Suppose the murderer takes the shouting and arm waving to be great

enthusiasm over the fact that he rid the town of a scoundrel;
he transmutes the anger into enthusiastic approval. Walk-
ing downstairs to acknowledge the ovation he suddenly
encounters anger in all its physicalness as he is unceremoni-
ously lynched.

> Also the eternal object may be the datum of a reverted
> conceptual feeling, only indirectly derived from the
> members of the original nexus. In this case, the trans-
> muted feeling of the nexus introduces novelty; and
> in unfortunate cases this novelty may be termed
> 'error.' [PR 387]

But also, "Error is the price which we pay for progress"
(PR 284), since "the approach to intellectuality consists
in the gain of a power of abstraction" (PR 388). Transmutation provides abstraction and is, consequently, essential
to the "approach to intellectuality." But a full understanding of the metaphysical characteristics of intellectuality
requires an analysis of phase IV of concrescence.

v. Phase IV of Concrescence

The circle *d*, in Figure 1 (above, page 56), represents a
complex comparative feeling, also called an intellectual
feeling. Consciousness is an eternal object embodied in
the subjective form of an intellectual feeling. For consciousness to arise as the subjective form of a feeling, that feeling
must prehend a special sort of datum. The characteristics of
such a datum are indicated by bracket *z* in Figure 1.

> In an intellectual feeling the datum is the generic
> contrast between a nexus of actual entities and a
> proposition with its logical subjects members of the
> nexus. In every generic contrast its unity arises from
> the two-way functioning of certain entities which are

components in each of the contrasted factors. [PR 407]

The first element of the contrast, the element referring to the real fact, is indicated by the lower leg of bracket z which stretches back to a. The second element of the contrast, the element referring to propositional abstraction, is indicated by the upper leg of bracket z which points to c, and through c to the proposition which is the datum for c. The diagram clearly exhibits the two-way functioning of a within the generic contrast which is the datum for d; a constitutes the logical subject of the proposition generated by a and b, and also constitutes the nexus of actual occasions, or the actual occasion as the case may be, contrasted with the proposition in the more sophisticated feeling at d.

But while a exhibits a two-way functioning in d, a enters into the two legs of the bracket z in different manners. In the lower leg it enters in full concreteness. In the upper leg it enters, as logical subject of the proposition y, in abstraction: [10]

10. John W. Blyth, in his study *Whitehead's Theory of Knowledge* (Providence, Brown University, 1941), develops in minute detail Whitehead's theory of propositions. Blyth attempts to draw out a major inconsistency in Whitehead on this very point of the two-way functioning of a (see his chap. 9, especially pp. 82–84). The alleged inconsistency arises from a supposed violation of Category of Explanation xxvi. I would maintain that there is no inconsistency because the "final satisfaction" has not yet been reached at this point; there is no Categoreal Demand for a to have only one function at a stage *prior* to the final satisfaction. Whitehead makes it clear that the "affirmation-negation contrast" is what ensures unity of function of a from the perspective of the final satisfaction: "In an intellectual feeling the datum is the generic contrast between a nexus of actual entities and a proposition with its logical subjects members of the nexus. . . . The common 'subject' entertaining the two feelings effects an integration whereby each of these actual entities obtains its one rôle of a two-way functioning in the one generic contrast. . . . Thus what in origination is describable as a pair of distinct ways of func-

in a proposition the logical subjects are reduced to the status of food for a possibility. Their real rôle in actuality is abstracted from; they are no longer factors in fact, except for the purpose of their physical indication. Each logical subject becomes a bare '*it*' among actualities, with *its* assigned hypothetical relevance to the predicate. . . . [The] peculiar objectification of the actual entities, really effected in the physical feeling, is eliminated, except in so far as it is required for the services of the indication. The objectification remains only to indicate that definiteness which the logical subjects must have in order to be hypothetical food for that predicate. [PR 394]

The two types of simple comparative feelings capable of appearing at *c* in Figure 1 can now be precisely distinguished. The first, more primitive type are physical purposes; the second, more developed type are propositional feelings. The distinction involves the reduction of the objective datum at *a* into a multiplicity of bare logical subjects, a bare "it," at *c*. Physical purposes do *not* carry out this reduction, hence they do not serve as lures for further comparative integration:

In such a type of physical purposes the integration of a physical feeling and a conceptual feeling does not involve the reduction of the objective datum of the physical feeling to a multiplicity of bare logical subjects. The objective datum remains the nexus that it is, exemplifying the eternal objects whose ingression constitutes its definiteness. Also the indeterminate-

tioning of each actual entity in the two factors of the generic contrast respectively, is realized in the subject as one rôle with a two-way aspect" (PR 407). See PR 347, and William A. Christian, *An Interpretation of Whitehead's Metaphysics* (New Haven, Yale University Press, 1959), pp. 25–26.

ness as to its own ingressions is eliminated from the eternal object which is the datum of the physical feeling [as it sinks back from its transcendent state at *b* into integration with itself as immanent at *c*]. [PR 421]

It is the reduction of the objective datum to a multiplicity of bare logical subjects in a propositional feeling which prevents the elimination of indefiniteness characteristic of the eternal object at b, even in the contrast at c, and this retention of indefiniteness is what serves as a lure for the feeling that arises at d with consciousness as an element in its subjective form.[11]

In an interesting passage Whitehead relates his technical account of consciousness to the facts of ordinary conscious experience:

> This account agrees with the plain facts of our conscious experience. Consciousness flickers; and even at its brightest, there is a small focal region of clear illumination, and a large penumbral region of experience which tells of intense experience in dim apprehension. The simplicity of clear consciousness is no measure of the complexity of complete experience. Also this character of our experience suggests that consciousness is the crown of experience, only occasionally attained, not its necessary base. [PR 408]

All the machinery necessary to introduce the distinctions between the various types of intellectual feelings has now been presented. The differences among the various types of intellectual feelings at *d* are determined by the differences among the various types of propositional feelings at *c* that form one element in the intellectual con-

11. I emphasize this point, not only because it is essential if one would grasp the difference between physical purposes and propositional feelings, but also because the distinction plays an important role in the aesthetic theory of Part II, below.

trast. Propositional feelings are divided into two major
categories each of which results in intellectual feelings of
a distinctive type. The two major categories of propositional feelings are (1) perceptive propositional feelings,
resulting in the species of intellectual feelings termed "conscious perceptions"; and (2) imaginative propositional feel-

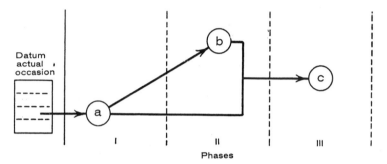

Figure 5. Perceptive Propositional Feeling

ings resulting in the species of intellectual feelings termed
"intuitive judgments." The genesis of perceptive propositional feelings, and hence of conscious perceptions, is
indicated in Figure 5. The genesis of imaginative propositional feelings, and hence of intuitive judgments, is indicated in Figure 6. In Figure 5 the physical feeling *a* (termed
the "indicative feeling") that points out the logical subjects is identical with the physical feeling that involves the
eternal object *b* (termed the "physical recognition") which
is to be contrasted with *a* at *c*. In Figure 6, however, the
indicative feeling *a* is *not* identical with the physical recognition *m* which involves the eternal object *n* to be contrasted at *c* with the indicative feeling *a*. In the case of the
imaginative propositional feeling of Figure 6, the two datum actual occasions α and β may be (1) so much alike
that an intellectual feeling (an intuitive judgment) based
on them is quite true, (2) sufficiently different so that an

intellectual feeling based on them is false, or (3) so diverse that the intuitive judgment formed is neither affirmative nor negative, but is quite indifferent to truth or falsehood, as when a fairy tale begins with the phrase "once
upon a time." This latter is an instance of conscious imagination.

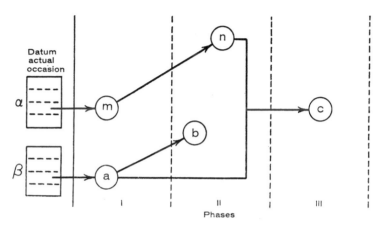

Figure 6. Imaginative Propositional Feeling

It may appear at this point as though perceptive propositional feelings must always be true. Perceptive propositional feelings, however, can be divided into two categories,
those that are authentic and those that are unauthentic. Figure 5, in fact, portrays an authentic perceptive
propositional feeling; Figure 7 portrays, by way of contrast, an unauthentic perceptive propositional feeling. Here
the novel element is *b'*, derived from *b* by means of a reversion. If *b* happened to be blue and were reverted at *b'*
into black, the conscious perception at *d* (Figure 1) resulting from this unauthentic perceptive propositional feeling
c would not be true, i.e. the predicate would not have
realization in the nexus. It should be noted that there is
a great similarity between Figures 6 and 7. Whitehead spe-

cifically notes the similarity and at one point (PR 401) describes unauthentic perceptive propositional feelings as "tied imagination," since the novelty is tied to one physical basis, one ultimate fact, and not spread out (as portrayed in Figure 6) between two physical facts as happens in conscious imagination.

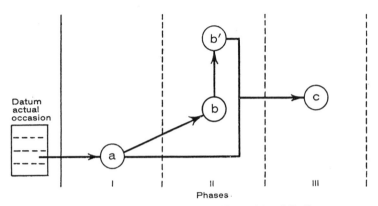

Datum
actual
occasion

Phases

Figure 7. Unauthentic Perceptive Propositional Feeling

The authentic perceptive propositional feelings (Figure 5) are true with just one further qualification. This qualification involves not the subject actual occasion in the process of concrescence, but the actual entity which is its datum.[12] If this datum actual occasion has initiated a maverick conceptual reversion (say it felt something physically as blue but conceptually reverted it to black), the possibility remains that its maverick reversion, which *is* something that has realization in that datum *ideally*, might be *transmuted* by the concrescing subject so that the maverick reversion appears to have realization in that datum *physically*. If the concrescing subject fails to understand what happened,

12. It might help to refer here to the structure of the datum actual occasion, in Fig. 3, p. 60.

error arises. An authentic perceptive propositional feeling is said to be "direct" when there is either no reversion in the datum actual occasion, or no transmutation in the subject to cause obscuring of that reversion.[13] A direct authentic perceptive propositional feeling is, without qualification, true.

VI. SATISFACTION

A few remarks about the "satisfaction" of an actual entity will conclude this account of concrescence.[14] Category of Explanation xxv reads:

> The final phase in the process of concrescence, constituting an actual entity, is one complex, fully determinate feeling. This final phase is termed the 'satisfaction.' It is fully determinate (a) as to its genesis, (b) as to its objective character for the transcendent creativity, and (c) as to its prehension—positive or negative—of every item in its universe. [PR 38]

13. Whitehead's exposition at PR 400–1 is not as clear as one might wish. Blyth, *Whitehead's Theory of Knowledge*, in a long footnote on p. 73, gives up and asserts that we have a contradiction "unless we assume that a typographical error has been made." The "contradiction" arises, he maintains, from defining authentic perceptive propositional feelings as involving no reversion on p. 400 of PR, and then on p. 401 maintaining that indirect authentic perceptive propositional feelings *do* involve reversion. As my exposition indicates, I think that Whitehead is saying that the reversion in an *indirect* authentic perceptive propositional feeling occurs *not* in the subject, or concrescing actual occasion, but in the *datum* actual occasion. There is hence no contradiction with the definition of an authentic perceptive propositional feeling as containing no reversion, since it is here the subject, not the datum, actual occasion to which reference is being made. My interpretation is substantiated, I believe, by the further discussion that occurs at PR 410. In particular, the italicized phrase *entertained in the nexus* leads one to believe that Blyth has given up too quickly.

14. Christian, *An Interpretation of Whitehead's Metaphysics*, pp. 21–46, provides a thorough analysis of the notion of the "satisfaction" of an actual occasion.

The satisfaction can be viewed as the solution to the basic problem which the concrescence must solve, i.e. how to unify the many components of the objective content "in one felt content with its complex subjective form" (PR 233).

> In the conception of the actual entity in its phase of satisfaction, the entity has attained its individual separation from other things; it has absorbed the datum, and it has not yet lost itself in the swing back to the 'decision' whereby its appetition becomes an element in the data of other entities superseding it. Time has stood still—if only it could. [PR 233] [15]

But time cannot stand still; hence the satisfaction

> is the outcome separated from the process, thereby losing the actuality of the atomic entity, which is both process and outcome . . . [The] 'satisfaction' is the 'superject' rather than the 'substance' or the 'subject.' It closes up the entity; and yet is the superject adding its character to the creativity whereby there is a becoming of entities superseding the one in question. [PR 129]

The satisfaction is the terminal unity of process, and as such it "embodies what the actual entity is beyond itself" (PR 335), i.e. it constitutes the character of the "decision" of that actual entity whereby it "adds a determinate condition to the settlement for the future beyond itself" (PR 227).

Concrescence presupposes, then, the settled actual world as datum; concrescence adds via process the individuality, the warmth, the vitality, the subjective involvement with which the concrescing subject clothes the dead datum

15. See PR 227, where Whitehead distinguishes four phases constitutive of an actual entity: datum, process, satisfaction, decision.

which is the "decision received" for it; the satisfaction emerges from the determinateness resulting from the individual vitality; and the "decision transmitted" is how that subject functions as superject, i.e. how it conditions the creativity that transcends it, how it exerts its "objective immortality," how it becomes dead datum that will be "decision received" for a fresh actual occasion.

4. Some Extensions of the System

THIS chapter will briefly elaborate some of the implications of the systematic framework which will be useful for Part II. Specifically, it will investigate the notions of nexus and society, and the doctrines of causal efficacy and presentational immediacy as they lead to an account of perception in the mode of symbolic reference. These doctrines will figure prominently in the early sections of Chapter 7.

1. Nexus and Society

The account of transmutation in Chapter 3 noted the mechanics of the process whereby a nexus arises as the datum for a transmuted physical feeling. It was pointed out that for transmutation to occur there must arise in the concrescing subject occasion a single conceptual feeling which refers impartially to all the physical feelings that that subject has of the individual actual entities which constitute that nexus. For this single impartial conceptual feeling to arise, the eternal object which is the datum of that conceptual feeling has to be somehow present—conceptually, physically, or via similar reversions—in a great majority of the actual occasions constitutive of that nexus. A nexus is felt as a nexus only as a result of transmutation, but for transmutation to occur there must be a concrete involvement, a uniformity, a mutual relatedness holding among the actual entities which go to make it up.

Actual entities involve each other by reason of their prehensions of each other. There are thus real individual facts of the togetherness of actual entities, which are real, individual, and particular, in the same sense in which actual entities and the prehensions are real, individual, and particular. Any such particular fact of togetherness among actual entities is called a 'nexus' (plural form is written 'nexūs'). [PR 29–30]

The fact that the same eternal object is present in a great majority of the members of a nexus results from the fact that these member actual entities are "involved" with each other "by means of their prehensions of each other."

This phrase "of each other" is ambiguous and unfortunate; it has led commentators to assume that Whitehead's doctrine of nexūs is incompatible with other aspects of his philosophy. John Blyth, for instance, equates "prehensions of each other" with "mutual prehensions" and therefore quite understandably writes:

> the concept of a nexus as defined above is illegitimate in Whitehead's system, for there can be no mutual prehension between actual entities. It was seen above that for one actual entity to be prehended by another it must be antecedent to the prehending entity and must be prehended in virtue of its antecedence. Now obviously two actual entities cannot possibly be antecedent to each other. Consequently, two or more actual entities cannot be united in a nexus by their prehensions of each other. This is true not only for contemporary actual entities which are causally independent of one another but also for entities which stand in different temporal relations to each other. It is therefore impossible for Whitehead to introduce any order into his universe in terms of nexūs.[1]

1. Blyth, *Whitehead's Theory of Knowledge*, p. 18. Blyth goes on to

Blyth is impeccably correct in asserting (a) that an actual occasion can only prehend antecedent actual occasions and (b) that contemporary actual occasions are causally independent, i.e. they are none of them prehended by any other. In fact, Whitehead defines past, present, and future in terms of these prehensive relationships. These relationships will be considered again in the discussion of presentational immediacy; at the moment the notion of a nexus needs to be rescued.

Figure 8 is a two-dimensional diagram representing a four-dimensional nexus. A given horizontal rung of Figure 8 at any level represents a three-dimensional, sagittal slice through time, dividing it into earlier and later. It also represents a bevy of contemporary actual occasions. The vertical dimension adds time; it represents generations of actual entities succeeding one another. The entire diagram represents a nexus. The subscript level 2 might be considered as my chair this morning and the subscript level 5 might be that same chair just a short while ago. The chair is the same chair it was, not because it is composed of the same identical actual occasions as it was this morning, but because now, this morning, and yesterday it is all one nexus.

---

remark that "these difficulties . . . render the entire system initially unplausible." In Chap. 3, above, I have shown that two of Blyth's criticisms of Whitehead are unfounded. I shall do the same here and once again at the end of this chapter. In my introductory chapter I noted that some commentators have argued that Whitehead's metaphysics suffers from deep-seated inconsistencies that vitiate its metaphysical usefulness. Blyth is taking this tack in arguing that the problems he finds "render the entire system initially unplausible." By taking issue with him, I do not mean to suggest that his book can therefore be dismissed—it contains many points that need to be wrestled with. But in refuting certain of his contentions I hope to dispel some of the pessimism with which he views Whitehead's system and to encourage further attempts to clarify, or rework, the Whiteheadian categories where needed in an effort to achieve maximum coherence as an ever firmer foundation for demonstrated applicability.

At 6, I ripped one leg off the chair. The contemporaries of the leg at 6 were not aware of what was happening, but at 7 the entities prehended the situation and the whole nexus was affected accordingly. At the 8 and 9 level the same nexus persists, but it is modified since the relationship of prehensions is now different. The modification is

A_1	B_1	C_1	D_1
A_2	B_2	C_2	D_2
A_3	B_3	C_3	D_3
A_4	B_4	C_4	D_4
A_5	B_5	C_5	D_5
A_6	B_6	C_6	D_6
A_7	B_7	C_7	
A_8	B_8	C_8	
A_9	B_9	C_9	

Figure 8. Nexus

indicated by the superscript. Sometimes nexūs are modified imperceptibly, as when a mountain erodes through the ages; sometimes nexūs are modified violently, as when a volcanic eruption causes an island chain to disappear beneath the sea.

In Figure 8, B_4 prehends all the occasions on the 3, 2, and 1 levels; prehends, and is prehended by, none of the other actual occasions at the 4 level; and is prehended by, or is an objectification for, all the 5's, 6's, 7's, etc. B_4 objectifies C_3 from just about the same perspective from which B_3 objectified C_2, B_4 objectifies A_3 from just about the same perspective from which B_3 objectified A_2, and B_4 objectifies D_3 from just about the same perspective from which B_3 objectified D_2. B_4 experiences the relationship among A_3, C_3, and D_3 which B_3 had experienced among

A$_2$, C$_2$, and D$_2$. A$_4$, C$_4$, and D$_4$ are all also experiencing the relationships among their immediate predecessors which those predecessors, as resident at the 3 level, had experienced as obtaining among their data at the 2 level. The result is a solid interweaving of perspectives such that if red happens to have been a dominant element in the subjective forms of the actual occasions involved at any point, red will tend to continue as a dominant element in successive stages of that nexus and transmutation will continue to occur when that nexus is prehended by suitably complex occasions.

The interlinking relationship of perspectives described in the above paragraph is meant to exhibit what Whitehead probably had in mind when he used the phrase "prehensions of each other." One might say that a group of children on a playground are all standing about looking at each other, and this would be a perfectly apt description even if it happens to be the case that no child is looking at the particular child who is looking at him. These considerations are sufficient to override Blyth's objection.[2]

Blyth has, however, correctly seen that it is via nexūs that Whitehead introduces order into his universe of monadic actual entities. When a nexus satisfies certain conditions, to be set forth immediately, it is said to exhibit social order and is called a society.[3]

2. I do not mean to imply that Blyth's objection is completely unfounded. Whitehead is careless in this connection. For example, he writes: "a physical feeling, belonging to the percipient, feels the nexus between two other actualities, A and B. It feels feelings of A which feel B, and feels feelings of B which feel A. It integrates these feelings, so as to unify their identity of elements. These identical elements form the factor defining the nexus between A and B . . ." (PR 351). Blyth is right in insisting that Whitehead cannot consistently say this about A and B, but my aim in the text has been to show that Whitehead need not have chosen this unfortunate way of explaining the notion of a nexus.

3. AI 258–67 constitutes a terse yet detailed account of Whitehead's doctrine of nexūs and societies.

Whitehead specifies very precisely the characteristics that generate social order:

> A nexus enjoys 'social order' where (i) there is a common element of form illustrated in the definiteness of each of its included actual entities, and (ii) this common element of form arises in each member of the nexus by reason of the conditions imposed upon it by its prehensions of some other members of the nexus, and (iii) these prehensions impose that condition of reproduction by reason of their inclusion of positive feelings of that common form. . . . the common form is the 'defining characteristic' of the society. . . . The reproduction of the common form throughout the nexus is due to the genetic relations of the members of the nexus among each other, and to the additional fact that genetic relations include feelings of the common form. Thus the defining characteristic is inherited throughout the nexus, *each member deriving it from those other members of the nexus which are antecedent to its own concrescence.* [PR 50–51, my italics] [4]

Genetic relations are those that hold in virtue of the prehensive character of actual occasions, i.e. relations arising from the fact that actual occasions can be analyzed into component prehensions (PR 334–35). It is crucial to Whitehead's system that "Apart from inhibitions or additions, weakenings or intensifications, due to the history of its production, the subjective form of a physical feeling is re-enaction of the subjective form of the feeling felt" (PR 362). Since, in the case of actual entities that compose the lower type societies, these inhibitions, additions,

---

4. The italicized passage supports the analysis above of the interlinking relationship of perspectives constitutive of a nexus. It also serves as a refutation of Blyth on this point.

weakenings, and intensifications are negligible, subjective forms at this level are, for practical purposes, almost complete re-enactions. This accounts for the "reproduction of the common form throughout the nexus." [5]

Societies do not exist in isolation, but nestle one inside another, each special society presupposing its social background. Journeying outward first, at a fairly high level of generality are found the "laws of nature," the order exhibited by the society of electronic and protonic actual entities that dominate our special cosmic epoch. But these electromagnetic occasions presuppose the order of even wider societies; the geometrical axioms, four-dimensionality, mere dimensionality, and finally the basic order of extensiveness (PR 140). As regards this most general society Whitehead writes: "In these general properties of extensive connection, we discern the defining characteristic of a vast nexus extending far beyond our immediate cosmic epoch. It contains in itself other epochs, with more particular characteristics incompatible with each other" (PR 148). The widest system of order, that of extensive connection, is such that it could tolerate within itself cosmic epochs quite incompatible with our own—one of seven dimensions constituted of anti-protonic and anti-electronic occasions, for instance.

Within the society of electronic and protonic occasions

5. I note in passing that Whitehead's somewhat unhappy use of the phrase "prehensions of each other" is the result of a desire to emphasize the difference between the nexus as society and a class. A class is what Whitehead technically terms a "mere multiplicity"; it is "held together" by an extremely weak type of order, a "merely mathematical conception of 'order' " (PR 137). A social nexus, on the other hand, is "self-sustaining" and "its own reason" because, "To constitute a society, the class-name has got to apply to each member, *by reason of genetic derivation from other members of that same society.* The members of the society are alike because, by reason of their common character, they impose on other members of the society the conditions which lead to that likeness" (PR 137, my italics). The order here is of a completely different kind from that which holds in a mere mathematical class. See also AI 261.

of our cosmic epoch, the order of which constitutes the laws of nature, are found societies exhibiting ever more and more special characteristics of order. Some of these more special societies exhibit personal order, i.e. their members are "arranged in a serial order by their genetic relations" (PR 138). Such a society is purely temporal, i.e. it "will include no pair of contemporary occasions" (AI 259). A personally ordered society is "a mere thread of temporal transition from occasion to occasion" (AI 259); spatial spread is completely lacking. Whitehead tentatively identifies the simplest personal societies with those historic routes of electronic (or protonic) actual entities that constitute the existence of electrons (or protons). Within a molecule there are many "strands," i.e. many routes of electronic and protonic occasions, each strand being a personally ordered society, also called by Whitehead an enduring object (PR 51). The molecule is, therefore, a "corpuscular society," or a "structured society."

> A nexus which (i) enjoys social order, and (ii) is analysable into strands of enduring objects may be termed a 'corpuscular society.' A society may be more or less corpuscular, according to the relative importance of the defining characteristics of the various enduring objects compared to that of the defining characteristic of the whole corpuscular nexus. [PR 52] [6]

A chair is a "complex" structured society, exhibiting an intricate structural pattern in respect to its many associated subordinate societies and subordinate nexūs.[7]

6. One naturally thinks of the difference in state-central government powers under the Articles of Confederation and again under the Constitution; with the strengthened central government the society became less corpuscular.

7. A sub-society is a society that could sustain itself apart from the parent structured society (an electron in the body, for instance), whereas a sub-nexus is a society, but a society that could not genetically sustain

Some members of very complexly structured societies enjoy great intensity of satisfaction because of the ordered complexity of contrasts which the other components in the society provide for them. In this way "the growth of a complex structured society exemplifies the general purpose pervading nature. The mere complexity of givenness which procures incompatibilities has been superseded by the complexity of order which procures contrasts" (PR 153). But such complex structured societies demand great stability of environment if they are to survive. There are accordingly two ways in which complex structured societies have solved the problem of achieving intensity and survival simultaneously: the way of inorganic bodies and the way of organic bodies. An inorganic body

> employs the device of blocking out unwelcome detail. It depends on the fundamental truth that objectification is abstraction. It utilizes this abstraction inherent in objectification so as to dismiss the thwarting elements of a nexus into negative prehensions. At the same time the complex intensity in the structured society is supported by the massive objectifications of the many environmental nexūs . . . [PR 154]

An organic, or living, body, on the other hand, does not block out novel elements, but relishes novelty, since it parries the potential destructiveness of that novelty by originating in its own subjective aim a novelty which will allow it successfully to match the novelty of the environment. It "deflects" the external novelty and, "This deflection in general originates a self-preservative reaction throughout the whole society. It may be unfortunate or inadequate; and in the case of persistent failure we are in

---

itself apart from the parent structured society (the brain, for instance). See PR 151–52, 163.

the province of pathology" (PR 156). It should be noted that the response of inorganic and organic bodies to the demands of simultaneous intensity and survival entails in both cases a scale of mentality "beyond the mere reproductive stage which employs nothing more than the Category of Conceptual Reproduction" (PR 155). The initiative of conceptual integration is present in inorganic bodies in virtue of the transmutation they accomplish, but the originality of reversion is present only in living adaptation to environment. Within a living body, however,

> only some of its [component] nexūs will be such that the mental poles of all their members have any *original* reactions. These will be its 'entirely living' nexūs, and in practice a society is only called 'living' when such nexūs are regnant [i.e. dominate the other sub-societies and sub-nexūs of the complex structured society]. [PR 157]

Entirely living nexūs require the protection of the rest of the complex structured society if they are to survive; hence, they are sub-nexūs and not sub-societies.[8]

> A complex inorganic system of interaction is built up for the protection of the 'entirely living' nexūs, and the originative actions of the living elements are protective of the whole system. On the other hand, the reaction[s] of the whole system provide the intimate environment required by the 'entirely living' nexūs. [PR 157]

This brief outline must suffice as a description of the emergence of different levels of order among actual occasions. It remains to adumbrate the account Whitehead gives of ordinary sense perception as experienced by liv-

8. See above, p. 79, n. 7.

ing, personally ordered societies, an account he refers to as the theory of symbolic reference.

II. SYMBOLIC REFERENCE

There are two pure modes of perception; the mode of causal efficacy and the mode of presentational immediacy. Symbolic reference is a mixed mode of perception resulting from a synthesis of the two pure modes. Many of the important features of both pure modes have already been introduced in previous discussions; explicit attention must now be given to these features and to the character of their interaction in symbolic reference.

The discussions of prehensions have actually presented a description of perception in the mode of causal efficacy. The experience of the simplest grades of actual occasions, deficient in the higher phases of concrescence, is an "unoriginative response to the datum with its simple content of sensa" (PR 176). The satisfaction of such a simple actual occasion, which merely re-enacts the satisfaction of its datum, is an instance of efficient causation;[9] only with the effectiveness of originative phases of concrescence does final causation become operative. Perception in the mode of causal efficacy is this direct, unadorned feeling of antecedent actual occasions which are efficacious as objectifications for the concrescing actual occasion.

In moving to consider perception in the mode of presentational immediacy it is important to note that "the transition from without to within the body marks the passage from lower to higher grades of actual occasions" (PR 183). Perception in the mode of causal efficacy is enjoyed by the most rudimentary actual occasion; perception in the mode of presentational immediacy presupposes the

9. Whitehead writes that in such simple occasions "the process is deficient in its highest phases; the process is the slave to the datum" (PR 176).

more elementary perception in the mode of causal efficacy and builds upon it through an application to it of the categories that emerge into relevance with the presence of higher phases of concrescence. These higher phases come into prominence only among actual occasions enmeshed in the ordered relationships enjoyed by members of highly complex structured societies.

The dominant characteristic of higher grades of actual occasions is, as has been shown, to take the eternal objects which emerge at b of Figure 1 (above, page 56) and, instead of allowing them to sink back in uncontrasted unity with a at c, as occurs in a physical purpose, rather holding them more and more aloof from a and thereby enhancing their significance in the final contrast with a. In this process the relevance of sensa is tremendously heightened. The culmination of this enhancement of sensa is the "givenness" for the percipient actual occasion of clearly articulated sensa, located in a geometrically specified contemporary region. This "givenness" of the sensa is the perception, in the mode of presentational immediacy, of the region illustrated by the sensa. But it is to be noted that the "givenness" of the sensa does not depend upon a donation by the contemporary spatial object which is presented by means of presentational immediacy; the donor is rather an object prehended in the mode of causal efficacy, and the contemporary spatial object is "given" as the result of a projection. A reconsideration of causal efficacy will reveal the mechanism responsible for the projection.

In Whitehead's system "it is a primary doctrine that what is 'given' is given by reason of objectifications of actual entities from the settled past" (PR 260). The sensa in question must, therefore, be donated to the percipient by past actual occasions. These sensa arise from the prehension, i.e. from the perception in the mode of causal efficacy, of actual occasions in the objectified past of the contemporary region to be illuminated by presentational immediacy. But the sensa thus prehended are not prehended in isolation. As prehended they are eternal objects of the subjective species that have been "objectified" long ago via transmutation and are currently being transmitted as objective data. They are eternal objects of the subjective species functioning in their secondary role. These eternal objects of the subjective species are prehended as interrelated with certain eternal objects of the objective species, with certain schemes of geometrical relationships. In the datum for the percipient

> there are first these components of . . . sensa combined with geometrical relationships to the external world of the settled past: secondly, there are also in the datum the general geometrical relationships forming the completion of this potential scheme into the contemporary world, and into the future. [PR 260–61]

The sensa are prehended as involved with geometrical patterns, and most important for present purposes, as involved with schematic extensions of these geometrical patterns which indicate the potential patterns for ingression of the sensa in future waves of actual occasions which will extend the temporal dimension of the nexus exemplifying the sensa. In terms of Figure 8 (above, page 75), imagine a percipient actual occasion, X_3, which does not appear in the diagram but is a contemporary of A_3, B_3, C_3, and D_3, and which prehends A_2, B_2, C_2, and D_2 as exhibiting, in addition to whatever sensa are involved, a geometrical relationship among A_2, B_2, C_2, and D_2 such that they outline a rectangle and A_2 and C_2 and B_2 and D_2 are joined by the diagonals. In the datum for X_3 is included, therefore, the general schema of relationships which holds between A_2, B_2, C_2, and D_2 plus a feeling for the geometrical "direction" which will be taken by these components of the total nexus as the nexus expands into its temporal dimension. This feeling for the geometrical direction of the nexus by X_3 will depend also on its inheritance from X_2 and X_1, which had prehended the nexus at successively antecedent states, and, so to speak, constitute "fixes" on the nexus. This feeling of geometrical direction, arising as a result of successive fixes on a nexus, is what Whitehead calls a "strain feeling." Supposing that the nexus concerned is a rectangular grey stone, the mechanism by which X_3 perceives A_3, B_3, C_3, and D_3 in the mode of presentational immediacy can be succinctly described as follows:

> The responsive phase [of X_3] absorbs these data [the sensa plus the geometrical relationships] as material for a subjective unity of feeling: the supplemental stage [of X_3] heightens the relevance of the colour-sensa, and supplements the geometrical relationships of the past by picking out the contemporary region of the stone to be the contemporary representative of the efficacious historic routes. There then results in the mode of presentational immediacy, the perception of the region illustrated by the sensum termed 'grey.' [PR 261]

It must be emphasized that all that perception in the mode of presentational immediacy reveals is "grey there now."

> What is directly perceived, certainly and without shadow of doubt, is a grey region of the presented locus. Any further interpretation, instinctive or by intellectual judgment, must be put down to symbolic reference. [PR 261]

As indicated, symbolic reference is a judgment; it is a putting together of two elements to make one whole. The two elements joined are perception in the mode of causal efficacy and perception in the mode of presentational immediacy. Figure 1 enables us to visualize what is happening, because, as noted, symbolic reference is a judgment and *d* in the figure is the locus of judgments; *z*, which indicates the data for *d*, reaches back to *a*, to perception in the mode of causal efficacy. The upper leg of bracket *z* reaches back to *c*. At *c* the sensa inherited from *b* have been heightened in relevance for the concrescing actual occasion. The pinnacle of enhancement achieved at *c* by actual occasions of the highest order is a lifting of the past into the present, a lifting into "distinct, prominent, relevance" in the mode of presentational immediacy of sensa but vaguely felt in the mode of causal efficacy. The final synthesis occurs at *d*; the heavy, vague feeling of efficacy associated with a prehended nexus has superimposed upon it the brilliant clarity of distinct regions exhibiting sensa. This superimposition is more than the sum of the two more primitive modes of perception, more than a mere reference from one mode to another; it is one unified mode of perception, the mixed mode of perception, i.e. symbolic reference. It has a metaphysical unity corresponding to the unity of everyday perceptual encounters with stones and trees:

> in fact, our process of self-construction for the achievement of unified experience produce[s] a new product, in which percepta in one mode, and percepta in the other mode, are synthesized into one subjective feeling. For example, we are perceiving before our eyes a grey stone [PR 271–72]. . . . The integration of the two modes in supplemental feeling makes what would have been vague to be distinct, and what would have been shallow to be intense. [PR 273]

As might be expected from previous discussions of Figure 1, as a fourth phase operation, symbolic reference can be the locus of error. Whitehead notes: "Such perception can be erroneous, in the sense that the feeling associates regions in the presented locus with inheritances from the past, which in fact have not been thus transmitted into the present regions" (PR 274). In his theory the bodily organs play a crucial role in two ways in that they transmit the physical inheritance from the past and also transmit the feelings of geometrical facts of order, the "strain feelings," which constitute the ground for projection in the mode of presentational immediacy. Should the bodily mechanism be even slightly disordered, as happens when one overindulges in alcoholic beverages or suffers from excessive emotional strain, for instance, then the deliverances of symbolic reference may well have little or no relevance to the future efficacy of the actual external environment.[10]

10. Blyth writes, p. 84: "Perhaps one of the most serious defects in Whitehead's theory of perception considered as a whole is his failure to coordinate the explanation of conscious perception with the two unconscious modes of perception." I don't believe this charge will stand up after serious investigation. I have purposely presented my account of symbolic reference in terms of Figure 1 to indicate that symbolic reference is quite compatible with the categories used to describe concrescence, and the emergence in concrescence of consciousness. At least part of Blyth's inadequacy here stems from a misunderstanding concerning the data of the two modes. Speaking of the modes of causal efficacy and presentational immediacy respectively, he writes, p. 86 (my italics): "and where the data of [the] one are past entities, *the data of the other are contemporary entities*." Building on this distinction, he then proceeds to argue that "Perceptions in the mode of presentational immediacy cannot then function in the origin of conscious feelings and cannot therefore contribute *their data, contemporary actual entities*, to the data of conscious feelings." It should be clear that the *data* of perceptions in the mode of presentational immediacy are *not* contemporary actual entities. Blyth is playing loose with the precisely defined notion of a "datum," as my discussion above of the "donation" of sensa for presentational immediacy tries to

This completes Part I of the book. A discussion of the formative elements preceded a detailed analysis of the phases of concrescence and in conclusion certain extensions of the basic system were noted. These sections have developed the Whiteheadian notions to be utilized by the aesthetic theory of Part II. I will turn now to a consideration of how these categories may be utilized to approach five traditional problems of aesthetic theory: a characterization of the aesthetic object, an account of aesthetic experience, a description of artistic creation, an explication of artistic truth, and an explanation of the function of art.

---

make clear; see also PR 260. Contemporary actual entities cannot be prehended by—i.e. cannot be a datum for—*any* feeling, be it conscious or unconscious; but perceptions in the mode of presentational immediacy *can* enter into conscious feelings because their data—i.e. the donors of their sensa—are *past* actual entities. See Christian, *Whitehead's Metaphysics*, p. 121, where an account of projection concludes that, "There is no need for any direct connection between A and its contemporaries to explain A's experience of a contemporary region."

Part II

AESTHETIC THEORY

5. Metaphor and Explanation:

An Introduction to the Aesthetic Theory

ARTISTS frequently pause in their work to wonder precisely what is happening when they themselves are creating: what is the nature and source of their inspiration? What is the peculiar nature of the objects they are creating which makes them aesthetic? How do these objects make their impact on those who contemplate them? In what sense do these objects embody truth? What is the purpose of creation, the function of art? The results of such reflection are invariably couched in metaphor, but nevertheless, such metaphors are extremely valuable as points of departure in the quest for a more precise, metaphysical understanding of aesthetic categories. E. M. Forster, in his tongue-in-cheek essay of 1925, "Anonymity: An Enquiry," [1] provides one such metaphor which is perceptive, lively, and typical of many such efforts at self-analysis. As an excuse for airing his thoughts, Mr. Forster is arguing the thesis that all real literature "tends towards a condition of anonymity, and that, so far as words are creative, a signature merely distracts us from their true significance." [2] He is led to an analysis of personality.

1. London, Leonard and Virginia Woolf at the Hogarth Press, 1925. From *Two Cheers for Democracy* (New York, Harcourt, Brace, 1951), by permission of the publishers.
2. Ibid., pp. 14–15.

Just as words have two functions—information and creation—so each human mind has two personalities, one on the surface, one deeper down. The upper personality has a name. It is called S. T. Coleridge, or William Shakespeare, or Mrs. Humphrey Ward. It is conscious and alert, it does things like dining out, answering letters, etc., and it differs vividly and amusingly from other personalities. The lower personality is a very queer affair. In many ways it is a perfect fool, but without it there is no literature, because, unless a man dips a bucket down into it occasionally he cannot produce first-class work. There is something general about it. Although it is inside S. T. Coleridge, it cannot be labelled with his name. It has something in common with all other deeper personalities, and the mystic will assert that the common quality is God, and that here, in the obscure recesses of our being, we near the gates of the Divine. It is in any case the force that makes for anonymity. As it came from the depths, so it soars to the heights, out of local questionings; as it is general to all men, so the works it inspires have something general about them, namely beauty. . . . What is so wonderful about great literature is that it transforms the man who reads it towards the condition of the man who wrote, and brings to birth in us also the creative impulse. . . .

If we glance at one or two writers who are not first class this point will be illustrated. Charles Lamb and R. L. Stevenson will serve. Here are two gifted, sensitive, fanciful, tolerant, humorous fellows, but they always write with their surface-personalities and never let down buckets into their underworld. Lamb did not try: bbbbuckets, he would have said, are bbeyond me, and he is the pleasanter writer in consequence. Stevenson was always trying oh ever so hard, but the bucket either stuck or else came up again full of the

R. L. S. who let it down[,] full of the mannerisms, the self-consciousness, the sentimentality, the quaintness which he was hoping to avoid. He and Lamb append their names in full to every sentence they write. They pursue us page after page, always to the exclusion of higher joy. They are letter writers, not creative artists, and it is no coincidence that each of them did write charming letters. A letter comes off the surface: it deals with the events of the day or with plans: it is naturally signed. Literature tries to be unsigned. And the proof is that, whereas we are always exclaiming "How like Lamb!" or "How typical of Stevenson!" we never say "How like Shakespeare!" or "How typical of Dante!" We are conscious only of the world they have created . . . The demand that literature should express personality is far too insistent in these days, and I look back with longing to the earlier modes of criticism where a poem was not an expression but a discovery, and was sometimes supposed to have been shown to the poet by God. . . . Imagination is our only guide into the world created by words. Whether these words are signed or unsigned becomes, as soon as the imagination redeems us, a matter of no importance, because we have approximated to the state in which they were written, and there are no names down there, no personality as we understand personality, no marrying or giving in marriage. What there is down there—ah, that is another enquiry, and may the clergymen and the scientists pursue it more successfully in the future than they have in the past.[3]

As an artist, and as one who lives with art, Mr. Forster has had wide aesthetic experience. He has here crystallized that experience metaphorically. But he is aware that he

3. Ibid., pp. 16–18, 23.

has not provided an explanation, a reasoned account. "What is down there"—that is indeed another inquiry, the inquiry that constitutes Part II of the present book.

T. E. Hulme has commented upon the widespread tendency to express insights concerning the arts metaphorically:

> I remember hearing Mr. Rothenstein in an after-dinner speech say that "art was the *revelation of the infinite in the finite*." I am very far from suggesting that he invented that phrase, but I quote it as showing that he evidently felt that it did convey something of the matter. And so it does in a way, but it is so hopelessly vague. It may convey the kind of excitement which art may produce in you, but it in no way fits the actual process that the artist goes through. It defines art in much the same way that saying that I was in Europe would define my position in space. It includes art, but it gives you no specific description of it.[4]

Forster's metaphor is not quite so unrevealing as Mr. Rothenstein's, but in its own way it is also "hopelessly vague." To eliminate at least some of this vagueness is my aim in the chapters that follow. They will seize upon certain aspects of the Forster metaphor and attempt to provide them with a precise interpretation within the systematic framework of Whitehead's metaphysical speculation. Chapter 6 will consider the question of the ontological status of the aesthetic object. Whitehead's theory of propositions will be utilized to specify the precise sense in which "the works [that the deeper personality] inspires have something general about them." Chapter 7 will analyze aesthetic experience. Whitehead's doctrine of prehensions will be used to specify the exact sense in which great art "transforms the man who [contemplates] it toward

4. *Speculations*, p. 148.

the condition of the man who [created it], and brings to birth in us also the creative impulse." Here the question of beauty will also be considered. Chapter 8 will discuss artistic creation. Whitehead's analysis of concrescence will generate a precise interpretation of such notions as "the underworld," "obscure recesses of our being," and "dips a bucket down." The sense in which God is a "common quality" and in which the creative artist draws "near the gates of the Divine" will also be specified. Forster's longing to conceive of a poem as a discovery will be taken into account at the same time that a proper use of the doctrine of "expression" is retained. Chapter 9, in considering the question of artistic truth, will specify one kind of answer for "what is down there." Finally, Chapter 10 will consider the function of art. Whitehead's arguments in *The Function of Reason* will lead to a theory of Art for Life's Sake, but a further analysis of the "world created by [art]" will isolate the elements of truth in the theory of Art for Art's Sake and unite them consistently with the former doctrine. These chapters are not isolated units; they are interdependent parts of a single aesthetic theory, each phase of which presupposes all the other parts. The selection of the order of presentation has been designed to exhibit this interdependence as strongly as possible.

Mr. Forster correctly recognizes that specialists other than the artist must provide the precise interpretations of the various aspects of his metaphor. There is a very real sense in which Plato was right in asserting that the poets do not "know" what they are doing. It can be added that it is not their business, as poets, to try and find out; it is enough if they simply do it. But philosophers are uneasy if they cannot understand the various dimensions of aesthetics more precisely than poets feel them in metaphor. This study aims at providing philosophical understanding.

The aesthetician, the philosopher dealing with the general problems of art, is not dealing merely with literary theory, or musical theory, or theory of painting. An aesthetician attempts to frame a theory which purports to say something true and interesting about all the arts. As a result the philosopher frequently finds himself attacked by the art critics, the literary critics, this particular poet, that painter. It is instructive to compare two papers read on the same platform at the Sanford Modern Language Meeting in 1949 by W. K. Wimsatt, Jr., and Theodore M. Greene.[5] Wimsatt's paper, titled "The Domain of Literary Criticism," begins: "The role which I have undertaken in this essay is that of defending the domain of poetry and poetics from the encircling (if friendly) arm of the general aesthetician." [6] Greene's reply to this somewhat less than friendly analysis is direct and convincing. He concludes his rebuttal, titled "The Scope of Aesthetics," with an excellent statement of his counterthesis:

> I hope this paper has made at least somewhat more plausible the thesis that the proper scope of aesthetics includes all works of art in all artistic media, whereas the proper domain of criticism is the interpretative understanding of specific works of art in this or that medium; that criticism must start with, and never lose sight of, what is distinctive in its medium, but, since it is dealing with *works of art* in this medium, that it cannot ignore with impunity any really adequate aesthetic principles it can devise or borrow from the aestheticians; and that the aestheticians, in turn, who of necessity must stand on the shoulders of the critics in all the media, must never forget that their aesthetic

5. Both papers are published in *Journal of Aesthetics and Art Criticism*, 8, June 1950. Wimsatt's article also appears as the first chapter of Section 4 in *The Verbal Icon*, New York, Noonday Press, paperbound edition, 1958.

6. *Journal of Aesthetics and Art Criticism*, 8, 213.

principles will certainly not be adequate, and will as certainly be harmful, to criticism, if they fail to do the fullest justice *both* to the common characteristics of all art as such, and *also* to the differentiae of the several arts in their very different artistic media. In short, I am convinced more than ever that a sound aesthetics and sound bodies of criticism are not enemies or rivals but mutually dependent allies in the common enterprise of interpreting art to the art lover, and of interpreting life, through the eyes of art, to mankind.[7]

I presuppose Greene's point of view in what follows. Part II of this essay is an attempt to develop categories relevant not only "to all works of art in all artistic media," but also to artistic creation in all artistic media and to the aesthetic experience of art objects in all artistic media. Everything which follows is written in the spirit of Greene's final exhortation to pursue "the common enterprise of interpreting art to the art lover, and of interpreting life, through the eyes of art, to mankind."

7. Ibid., p. 228.

6. The Aesthetic Object

In this chapter it will be argued that art objects have the ontological status of Whiteheadian propositions. Crucial to this argument is the distinction between works of art and their performances, which will be shown to be the distinction between propositions and their objectifications. This essay presents a general aesthetic theory, not a theory of this or that particular art. Therefore it will apply its doctrines to all the major arts: music, the dance, literature (including poetry and the theatre), architecture, painting, and sculpture. This application will involve distinguishing between the performer and the nonperformer arts. The theory of the aesthetic object which emerges will be shown to elucidate the phenomenon of Psychical Distance.

This chapter begins with some general reflections on the particular question of the ontological status of aesthetic objects. Since Whitehead's doctrine of propositions is central to the present theory of the aesthetic object, before presenting that theory, I summarize, and develop where required, the account of propositions given in Part I. The theory itself is then presented and discussed in terms of specific applications to the various arts.

1. Ontological Status

A classic discussion of the ontological status of a poem occurs in René Wellek and Austin Warren's *Theory of*

Literature.[1] In chapter 13, "The Analysis of the Literary Work of Art," they succeed in demonstrating that it is not a simple matter to specify what a poem is, where it is located, or how it exists. Reviewing their arguments will be helpful not merely as an introduction to the topic of this chapter, but also because certain points in their own positive theory parallel aspects of the present theory.

Wellek and Warren argue that the black lines of ink on paper (or, with a Babylonian poem, the grooves in the brick) cannot be the poem, since there are many poems in the oral literature which have never been fixed in writing yet still continue to exist.[2] Furthermore, the sort and size of type and page can vary without changing the poem and also the genuine meaning of a text can be restored by correcting errors on the printed page. Nor is the sequence of sounds uttered by a reader the poem. There is a written literature that may never be sounded at all, one can mentally correct errors in a reading, each reading adds elements extraneous to the poem, etc., etc. Nor can a poem be the experience of the reader; there would be as many Divine Comedies as readers and more, since one reader would not necessarily experience it the same in two separate readings. Nor is the poem the experience of the author, for this view leads to the many difficulties contained in the "Intentional Fallacy." Wellek and Warren, after dismissing these various ways of locating the literary work of art, conclude themselves that a poem

is not an individual experience or a sum of experiences, but only a potential cause of experiences. Definition in terms of states of mind fails because it cannot account for the normative character of the genuine poem, for the simple fact that it might be

1. New York, Harcourt, Brace, 1949.
2. Ibid., pp. 141 ff.

experienced correctly or incorrectly. In every individual experience only a small part can be considered as adequate to the true poem. Thus, the real poem must be conceived as a structure of norms, realized only partially in the actual experience of its many readers. Every single experience (reading, reciting, and so forth) is only an attempt—more or less successful and complete—to grasp this set of norms or standards.[3]

Even in their phraseology (for example, "a potential cause of experience") Wellek and Warren are very close to the notion of a Whiteheadian proposition, an impure potential which acts as a lure for feeling. The theory to be advanced here will exhibit their insights as emerging from Whitehead's brilliant speculative account of the nature of things. It also will eliminate the awkward and arbitrary characteristics of a view such as that of W. K. Wimsatt, Jr., who writes in the Introduction to *The Verbal Icon*:

> The poem conceived as a thing in between the poet and the audience is of course an abstraction. The poem is an act. The only substantive entities are the poet and the audience. But if we are to lay hold of the poetic act to comprehend and evaluate it, and if it is to pass current as a critical object, it must be hypostatized.[4]

Wimsatt's awkward necessity to hypostatize something that really isn't there is avoided in the present theory by recognizing that while indeed an abstraction, a poem is yet an existing entity whose mode of existence is in effect that of a specific kind of abstractness specifiable within a particular metaphysical theory.

3. Ibid., p. 151.
4. Wimsatt, *The Verbal Icon*, p. xvii.

Wellek and Warren's analysis has indicated that what might be an acceptable ontological theory for a painting or a statue will not necessarily serve to elucidate the nature of a poem, and they strongly imply that their analysis of the literary work of art is inapplicable to sculpture.[5] This raises the basic question of why all works of art need have the same ontological status. The student of literature, in trying to frame a theory of tragedy, searches for the common characteristics exhibited by all recognized tragedies. Likewise, in framing an aesthetic theory, the aesthetician looks for common characteristics exhibited by all recognized art objects. But there is no a priori reason why this common characteristic need be ontological status; it might just as well be function, for example. Some aestheticians have concentrated on the creative activity productive of works of art, attempting to find a common characteristic of art objects in the elements shared by artistic production in the various media. This tendency, however, has been discouraged by the contemporary school of analysis, which warns of the fundamental ambiguity of the word "art," citing the so-called "process-product" ambiguity.[6] This distinction is apparently designed to show that a theory of the aesthetic object is confused and inadequate if it depends upon or refers in any way to a theory of artistic creation. There is no question but that the word "art" can mean both the creating of aesthetic objects and the product of this creativity, and furthermore it is obvious that the two meanings of the word "art" should not be confused. But I submit that an aesthetic theory, to be adequate, must do justice to both senses of the word "art" and, what is most important, link these two senses in a

5. They write, for instance (p. 157): "The [literary] work of art, then, appears as an object of knowledge *sui generis* which has a special ontological status. It is neither real (like a statue) . . .' "

6. See Morris Weitz, *Problems in Aesthetics* (New York, Macmillan, 1959), p. 3.

meaningful relationship. Modern analyses for the most part do not satisfy this requirement because they rarely approach the stature of aesthetic theory, which requires integration, but are content with detailed, sharply restricted dissections of the use of words in one narrow range of sentences employed in discussing art objects. On the contrary, to the end of providing a genuine aesthetic theory, the present account indissolubly links its description of artistic creation to its description of the aesthetic object, and vice versa. It does this by specifying a unique ontological status for the work of art and linking that ontological status to its account of the characteristics of artistic creation. From this framework arises both a theory of aesthetic experience as artistic re-creation and an Art for Life's Sake theory of the function of art. The aesthetic theory of these chapters is one integrated theory. It is characteristic of this theory that it pivots about an account of the ontological status of aesthetic objects; this account is the cement that holds together the other elements constitutive of it. Since an account of the ontological status of the aesthetic object is, then, the essential aspect of this aesthetic theory, I shall turn immediately to a summary of the Whiteheadian theory of propositions upon which my own account of the ontological status of aesthetic objects depends.

II. The Theory of Propositions

A proposition is the objective datum of a propositional feeling (PR 391). A propositional feeling, it will be recalled from Chapter 3, is "a complex feeling derived from the integration of a physical feeling with a conceptual feeling" (PR 391). The datum of a conceptual feeling is an eternal object. A conceptual feeling is by itself completely general. Hence a conceptual feeling does not refer to *the* actual world, in the sense that the history of *this* actual world has any peculiar relevance to its datum. This datum is an eternal object; and an eternal object refers only to the purely general *any* among undetermined actual entities. In itself an eternal object evades any selection among actualities or epochs. [PR 391]

On the other hand, the datum of a physical feeling is either one actual entity or, if the feeling be complex, a determinate nexus of actual entities. This datum is unique and specific, a *this* as opposed to an *any*.

The propositional feeling arises from a "special type of integration synthesizing" these two types of more primitive feelings:

> In the integrated objective datum the physical feeling provides its determinate set of actual entities, indicated by their felt physical relationships to the subject of the feeling. These actual entities are the logical subjects of the proposition. The absolute generality of the notion of *any*, inherent in an eternal òbject, is thus eliminated in the fusion. In the proposition, the eternal object in respect to its possibilities as a determinant of nexus [nexūs], is restricted to these logical subjects. . . . The proposition is the potentiality of the eternal object, as a determinant of definiteness, in some determinate mode of restricted reference to the logical subjects. This eternal object is the 'predicative pattern' of the proposition. [PR 393]

In a proposition the predicative pattern loses its absolute generality, but the proposition as a whole preserves the indeterminateness of an eternal object. This is possible because the proposition makes an abstraction, albeit an in-

complete abstraction, from the side of the physical feeling;
it abstracts from the fully determinate actual entities which
are the datum of the component physical feeling. A logical
subject is not a fully concrete actual occasion; it is an abstraction. But it is an incomplete abstraction so that a
proposition still can be said to have

> determinate actual entities among its components.
> These determinate actual entities, considered *forma-
> liter* and not as in the abstraction of the proposition,
> do afford a reason determining the truth or falsehood
> of the proposition. But the proposition in itself, apart
> from recourse to these reasons, tells no tale about it-
> self; and in this respect it is indeterminate like the
> eternal objects. [PR 393]

The point to be emphasized, which will be central to the
subsequent aesthetic analysis, is that in a proposition the
logical subjects are not to be considered *formaliter*, but "as
in the abstraction of the proposition." [7] The status of these
logical subjects is so important to my purpose that I will
quote Whitehead at some length.

> In this synthesis [of eternal object and actual occasion
> within a proposition] the eternal object has suffered
> the elimination of its absolute generality of reference.
> The datum of the physical feeling has also suffered
> elimination. For the peculiar objectification of the
> actual entities, really effected in the physical feeling,
> is eliminated, except in so far as it is required for the
> services of the indication. The objectification remains
> only to indicate that definiteness which the logical
> subjects must have in order to be hypothetical food
> for that predicate. [PR 394]

7. It was noted above, p. 32, n. 22, that to speak of an actual occasion
formaliter is to speak of that occasion in the fullness of its own immediate
experience. Logical subjects of propositions have lost this immediacy.

And again:

> Thus in a proposition the logical subjects are reduced
> to the status of food for a possibility. Their real rôle
> in actuality is abstracted from; they are no longer fac-
> tors in fact, except for the purpose of their physical
> indication. Each logical subject becomes a bare '*it*'
> among actualities, with *its* assigned hypothetical rele-
> vance to the predicate. [PR 394]

In the preceding pages I have discussed propositions
and propositional feelings without having specified the
sharp difference between them. It was useful to introduce
the concept of a proposition through the mediation of the
concept of a propositional feeling; in effect I defined how
a proposition enters into experience as the datum of a
propositional feeling. This is a helpful heuristic device,
used by Whitehead himself, since in analyzing the individual data of the two component types of feelings integrated
in a propositional feeling we analyzed the components integral to a proposition. But lest this technique lead to a
misconception, propositions must now be exhibited in
their full independence as members of a unique category
of existence.

Whitehead writes: "In every proposition, as such and
without going beyond it, there is complete indeterminateness so far as concerns its own realization in a propositional
feeling, and as regards its own truth" (PR 394). Propositions stand on their own feet ontologically. They are not
dependent upon particular propositional feelings for their
existence, though by the ontological principle they "have
a reason" and ultimately this reason is the nontemporal
actual entity God. Rather than depending on propositional
feelings, propositions are presupposed by propositional feelings; a proposition is the lure urging a given prehending
subject to integrate one of its physical feelings with a con-

ceptual feeling so as to prehend positively that proposition as datum. The source of novelty in concrete actuality is a propositional feeling with the subjective form of adversion which results when a prehending subject entertains a proposition as a datum with the resolve to realize that proposition in concrete fact as an actual occasion. Whitehead deplores the exclusive interest shown by logicians in propositions as the data for judgments (PR 37, 395). It is basic to his philosophy to deny that the only important thing about propositions is their truth or falsity. Of prime importance is their interest, their effectiveness as lures. He insists that

> in the real world it is more important that a proposition be interesting than that it be true. The importance of truth is, that it adds to interest. The doctrine here maintained is that judgment-feelings form only one subdivision of propositional feelings; and arise from the special sort of integration of propositional feelings with other feelings. [PR 395–96]

A proposition, then, is one of Whitehead's eight categories of existence (PR 32–33). Whereas an eternal object is a pure potential for the specific determination of fact, a proposition is an impure potential for the specific determination of matters of fact. Both find their reasons for being in God.

> A proposition has neither the particularity of a feeling, nor the reality of a nexus. It is [a] datum for feeling, awaiting a subject feeling it. Its relevance to the actual world by means of its logical subjects makes it a lure for feeling. [PR 395]

He makes it clear in the following passage that a proposition is separate from the subject that prehends it as well as from any particular propositional feeling:

the physical feeling, which is always one component in the history of an integral propositional feeling, has no unique relation to the proposition in question, nor has the subject of that feeling, which is also a subject prehending the proposition. Any subject with any physical feeling which includes in its objective datum the requisite logical subjects, can in a supervening phase entertain a propositional feeling with that proposition as its datum. It has only to originate a conceptual feeling with the requisite predicative pattern as its datum, and then to integrate the two feelings into the required propositional feeling. [PR 396]

III. The Aesthetic Object as Proposition

The central contention that the remainder of this chapter will seek to establish is simply that aesthetic objects have the ontological status of Whiteheadian propositions. Subordinate to this theory are two corollaries essential to its development. The first is obtained by taking a terminological cue from Santayana's celebrated definition of beauty as "objectified pleasure"; [8] it will be argued that a performance of a work of art is an *objectified* proposition, in a sense to be specified. The second is that some of the arts are such as to permit an artist to set down in permanent form a set of rules, or instructions, to be used by performers in objectifying the proposition which is the work of art. An example of such a set of rules would be the musical score of *Kiss Me Kate* or a text of *King Lear*. It will be essential in what follows to preserve carefully the distinctions between works of art (or propositions), performances (or objectified propositions), and rules or instructions for the objectification of art objects.

I have said that only some of the arts are such as to permit an artist to set down in permanent form a set of rules,

8. *The Sense of Beauty* (New York, Modern Library, 1955), p. 54.

or instructions, to guide performers in the objectification of works of art. This qualification introduces the distinction between the performer arts and the nonperformer arts. By performer arts I mean literature, music, the dance, and architecture. In each of these arts there is a performer involved, whether that performer be a reader reading to himself, an actor on a stage, a symphony orchestra, a ballet company, or a commercial builder. The composer can certainly be a performer of his own works, as in the case of a Martha Graham or Franz Lizst. But there is an important difference, indicated by the presence of performers, between these four arts and the two nonperformer arts, painting and sculpture. A general aesthetics must account for this difference.

In the following discussion, which seeks to establish the plausibility and usefulness of the theory of propositions and its two corollaries, I will first discuss the theory as related to Edward Bullough's doctrine of Psychical Distance; secondly, will comment upon its application to, or exemplification in, the performer arts; and thirdly, will utilize architecture (which, though a performer art, shares some of the characteristics of the nonperformer arts) as a transition to a discussion of the nonperformer arts. I wish to emphasize that all of Part II constitutes a single unified theory. These initial comments will, it is hoped, prove interesting, but it is to be remembered that they are like the first occurrence of a major theme in a symphony; it is only after the other themes appear and share in the development that the first theme can reappear in its total significance at the recapitulation.

Psychical Distance

Edward Bullough's theory of Psychical Distance [9] has become a classic doctrine of aesthetic theory that must be

9. Edward Bullough, "Psychical Distance as a Factor in Art and an Aesthetic Principle," *British Journal of Psychology*, 5 (1912), 87–98.

taken into account by all aesthetic thinking. Indicating the manner in which the present theory provides a foundation for his insights will constitute an initial explication of the doctrine that the work of art has the ontological status of a Whiteheadian proposition.

A proposition is not an actuality; it is an impure potential. Its logical subject has its role in actuality abstracted from. Even as objectified a proposition is less than actual; it is this characteristic of objectifications, i.e. of performances, which supports the theory of Psychical Distance.

There is a difference between a street-knifing in Chicago and what happens in Shakespeare's *Julius Caesar*. One does not run onto the stage of a theater and rescue the heroine from the villain. Of course there is something actual about a performance of a play; the proposition which is the play is objectified by a concrete performal medium, which is actual. But the crucial point made by the doctrine of Psychical Distance is that it is catastrophic for aesthetic experience to identify the performal medium with the aesthetic object. This identification constitutes loss of Distance. It is the propositional character of art that renders it "distant" in Bullough's sense of the word.

Bullough catalogues the threats to Distance in the various arts with ingenuity and insight. In the case of the dance, for instance, he maintains there is apt to be an aesthetically disasterous loss of Distance if all too human impulses fail to be checked by "technical execution of the most wearing kind" and succumb to the "animal spirits" of the dancing.[10] On the theory here proposed this would amount to a concentration upon the performal medium used to objectify a proposition; one so guilty would be confusing the concrete actuality of the objectifying medium with the proposition objectified by that medium.

Gertrude Lippincott makes the same point in an even more illuminating way:

10. Ibid., p. 97.

> It is possible that the use of the body as the instrument of dance may . . . cause misunderstanding in the matter of representation, literal interpretation, and imitation. We are so close to the activities of the human body that we can not always *divorce ourselves from its actions and project ourselves into the realm of art, a realm which is out of the natural.*[11]

The italicized phrases are an appeal not to confuse the objectifying medium with the proposition objectified. The realm of art is the realm of the propositional, a realm not to be confused with the "natural," i.e. the actual. Bullough's insistence upon the need to "distance" works of art is paralleled by Miss Lippincott's statement as well as by the present demand that the work of art be recognized as propositional in character.

From even these few remarks it is apparent that the aesthetic theory I am developing has strong affinities with that of Benedetto Croce. Like Croce I argue that the art object is not an actual entity, but a thing of the spirit. But here and in what follows, rather than appropriating Croce's insights I am running them through the categories of Whitehead's system in such a way that they emerge with fresh value for aesthetic insight and firm metaphysical grounding in a philosophical system more adequate for our time than is that of Croce. Section 3 of Chapter 8 will indicate in detail the relation between the present theory and that of Croce in a climactic section that also binds together my accounts of the aesthetic object, aesthetic experience, and artistic creation. It is sufficient at the moment simply to point out the obvious parallel with Croce.

In Part I, and in section II of this chapter, propositions have been precisely defined in terms of actual occasions

11. "A Dancer's Note to Aestheticians," *Journal of Aesthetics and Art Criticism*, 8 (1949), 102. My italics.

and eternal objects. Yet these techncial discussions do not immediately indicate the correlation between propositions and everyday human experience. Having viewed works of art in terms of propositions, I must now turn about and suggest that everyday human experience of art objects can throw light on the nature of propositions. In illustrating the concept of psychical distance I have suggested that there is a difference between the assassination scene in *Julius Caesar* and a street-knifing in Chicago. The concrete experience of watching the play is an instance of prehending a proposition. We know that we are not witnessing an actual murder. We know that actually we are watching a group of men stab another man with rubber daggers; that is what actually transpires before our eyes. This knowledge is productive of Distance. But the actualities of the performal medium are not all that we prehend. What makes *Julius Caesar* a play and not a meaningless conglomeration of actualities is the proposition objectified in the performal medium. The point here is that we know what it is to experience *Julius Caesar;* hence this concrete example will suffice to illustrate what it is to apprehend a proposition—the example of the play correlates Whitehead's technical discussion of propositions with everyday first person experience. This example would be helpful in understanding Whitehead's metaphysics quite apart from the present interest in aesthetic problems. But given the aesthetic interest, the technical discussion of propositions can also help in understanding the nature of aesthetic objects.

Julius Caesar, Brutus, etc. constitute a nexus of logical subjects, subjects which have had their role in actuality abstracted from—"they are no longer factors in fact" (PR 394), "the peculiar objectification of the actual entities, really effected in the physical feeling, is eliminated" (PR 394). The play itself is not a physical entity, it is an ideal entity. In a performance of the play the objectification which has been eliminated in the ideal entity is restored; hence the performance is called an objectified proposition. But the objectification in the performance is second hand. An actual occasion is what it is; it does not persist, change, or reappear. Propositions can and do reappear in different performances because they are not actualities. Different actualities at different times and places, i.e. different acting companies, can serve as the objectifiers of a given proposition. Each company provides in its actors a group of actualities which objectify the proposition which is the play they perform. These actualities supply the objectification eliminated in the proposition which is the play itself. But it is the secondhandness of the objectification which they supply that Bullough refers to in his doctrine of Distance. Were the objectification immediate there would be a street-knifing and not the assassination of Julius Caesar in the play of that name.

These considerations will become more plausible as they are integrated into a theory of aesthetic experience and artistic creation. In particular the theory that aesthetic experience is the aesthetic re-creation by the contemplator of the proposition objectified in a performance compliments nicely the present theory and leads to a Whiteheadian formulation of Croce's view that the artifact, the objectification, is a means to achieve the end of permitting those who experience the objectification to reproduce the art object (proposition) in their own consciousness.

These points will be returned to and amplified in Chapters 7 and 8. At the moment they have served as introductory explications of the theory of the aesthetic object. This theory will now be developed further by a consideration of the characteristics of the performer and the non-performer arts.

The Performer Arts

In the discussion that follows I shall be using specific examples from the several performer arts: music, literature, the dance, and architecture. In general, remarks made about any one of these arts will be equally applicable to the others, *mutatis mutandis*. I shall frequently be drawing illustrative material from music in what follows and it may be wise to consider a special problem that arises in regard to music before proceeding further with a development of the general theory being presented. The problem is this: if the composition which is the work of art is a proposition, what could possibly be the logical subject of that proposition? In the case of a drama, a poem, or a ballet it is not very difficult to specify the logical subject or subjects, but in the case of music this seems to be a real problem. A friend once remarked to me that "all general theories of aesthetics are shipwrecked on the treacherous reef of musical facts." I don't think shipwreck is inevitable, but the danger is certainly there and must be faced up to.

In meeting this particular difficulty I take my cue from a certain class of very familiar propositions, the propositions expressed in ordinary imperative sentences. Every school child learns that the subject of an imperative sentence is "you" understood. What I want to suggest is that the logical subject of the proposition which is a musical composition is "you" understood, and I think I can show that this suggestion has interesting and fruitful implications.

Music is the most abstract of the arts, and for this reason has frequently been called the queen of the arts, the most pure of the arts, etc. But in what way is music abstract? Sounds are as concrete, as actual, as are the movements of a Julius Caesar or a Hamlet. I suggest that the sense in which music is abstract is relevant to the theory that the logical subject of the proposition which is a composition is "you" understood. Eduard Hanslick argues that music cannot represent specific feelings, such as love or fear.

> What part of the feelings, then, can music represent, if not the subject involved in them?
>
> Only their dynamic properties. It may reproduce the motion accompanying psychical action, according to its momentum: speed, slowness, strength, weakness, increasing and decreasing intensity. But motion is only one of the concomitants of feeling, not the feeling itself. . . . [Music] cannot reproduce the feeling of love but only the element of motion . . .[12]

Music represents, then, only a dynamic element of movement. In absolute music, as opposed to program music, I would contend that the logical subject of the music is "you" understood. The dynamic element is given, but the specific feeling to be correlated with the dynamic element is not. The listener must provide the feeling; his feeling is the subject of the proposition which is the composition. Only the predicative pattern is provided by the composer. As a result, in music more than in any other art the very nature of the art object is a function of the contemplator, since he provides the subject of the proposition which is the art object.

This suggestion is in keeping with several other valid points made by Hanslick in his classical study. He notes that "many of the most celebrated airs from *The Messiah*, including those most of all admired as being especially suggestive of piety, were taken from secular duets (mostly erotic) composed in the years 1711–1712, when Handel set to music certain madrigals by Mauro Ortensio for the

12. *The Beautiful in Music* (New York, Liberal Arts Press, 1957), p. 24.

Electoral Princess Caroline of Hanover." [13] Hanslick adds many other examples of this sort of ambiguity, even suggesting that when the *allegro fugato* from the overture to *The Magic Flute* is changed into "a vocal quartet of quarreling Jewish peddlars," the music "fits the low text appallingly well, and the enjoyment we derive from the gravity of the music in the opera can be no heartier than our laugh at the farcical humor of the parody." [14]

What conclusions can be drawn? They suggest that pure music in itself is merely predicative, that it conveys a dynamic element but does not specify the expressive nature of the psychical movement conveyed. Critics have argued endlessly about the specific feelings conveyed by a given piece of absolute music. Hanslick is surely right in insisting that such debate is bootless, and the reason is that each participant in the argument is equally entitled to provide the logical subject of the proposition, to provide the concrete element of feeling that the predicative pattern conveys only in its dynamic dimension. These facts also suggest that much music considered absolute has a decided programmatic tinge to it. Beethoven's dedication for the Third Symphony suffices to specify the logical subject of the proposition which is that symphony and remove it from the class of propositions whose logical subject is an unqualified "you" understood. The same holds for the Third Piano Concerto, and also for the "Moonlight Sonata"—it makes no difference, I suggest, whether the composer or a later generation affixes the programmatic element that establishes the logical subject of a composition; as long as the programmatic element sticks in public consciousness, the proposition which is involved has a specifiable subject, though the creative listener aesthetically recreating that proposition is free to assume the "you" under-

13. Ibid., p. 35.
14. Ibid., p. 34.

stood role and blind himself to the programmatic element, to his own greater joy or disappointment as the case may be.

These observations suggest that I am decidedly cool toward the doctrines of Art for Art's Sake, Significant Form, etc. It is true. I find that the *Weltanschauung* of Whitehead, his view of the world and man's place in it, fails to assimilate the aesthetic views of, for instance, Clive Bell and Hanslick (at least in some of his contentions). Bell's raptures over "pure art with a tremendous significance of its own and no relation whatever to the significance of life" [15] is both poor aesthetics and poor metaphysics. It just is not true that "to appreciate a work of art we need bring with us nothing from life, no knowledge of its ideas and affairs, no familiarity with its emotions." [16] In Chapter 10, below, I will exhibit my reasons for this view, but also specify a limited sense in which I can accept certain insights of the Art for Art's Sake theory. Surely it is the Art for Life's Sake doctrine of a writer like Iredell Jenkins [17] that is significant for aesthetics, and this I will argue in Chapter 10.

My comments on music fall into place in the light of this theory of the function of art. The doctrine that the work of art is a proposition, in its application to music, prepares the way for a theory of Art for Life's Sake. Traditionally, Art for Art's Sake theorists speak about music and abstract art while Art for Life's Sake theorists speak about the novel and the theater. The theory that the work of art is a proposition will enable me to bring music and abstract art within my discussion. Pure music is still in relationship with the world, Bell notwithstanding, because

15. *Art* (New York, Putnam, Capricorn Books, 1958), p. 30.
16. Ibid., p. 27.
17. See his *Art and the Human Enterprise*, Cambridge, Harvard University Press, 1958.

in absolute music the subject of the proposition which is a given composition is still "you" understood, entailing that the listener provides out of his worldly experience the concrete element of feeling that the predicative pattern conveys only in its dynamic dimension. Program music, of course, has a specifiable subject, and hence direct contact with the world.

These matters will come in for further discussion in the chapters that follow. I return from this digression now to a further development of the theory of the aesthetic object by means of a discussion of the performer arts.

An exploration of the relationship between artist and performer in the performer arts will serve to clarify some aspects of the present theory. A musical composition is a proposition. It has been prehended by the composer. The notes he sets down on staff paper, however, are not the work of art; they are, rather, a set of rules, or instructions, he prepares for the use of a performer. They are rules for objectifying a proposition. The proposition which is a given musical work has its own existence as a proposition, but is "encountered" by audiences only as objectified. It is impossible for the composer to specify exactly, in every detail, how the proposition is to be objectified. The rules of performance admit of some looseness and hence various interpretations of a given work are inevitable. In many cases the composer explicitly acknowledges his close collaboration with the performer by introducing into his composition a cadenza or a section marked "ad lib." In the literary arts one thinks of a rough parallel in the delightful spoofs called "Pantomimes" performed in London about Christmas time each year in which the actors have, in addition to set lines, great freedom to introduce relevant material from the day's headlines for irreverent comment. Ballet also allows ample opportunity for the individual dancer to indulge now and again in an original tour de force.

But the obvious fact of different interpretations of musical compositions does not break, or even weaken, the bond between a given proposition and its objectifications. That the proposition is there as a norm behind its objectifications is obvious; in this context Wellek and Warren's phrase "structure of norms" is a happy choice of words. Conductors recognize a bullseye toward which they aim as much as do archers. And it is surprising how close will be the judgment of critics as to a given conductor's success in hitting his target. The composition is there, it is a proposition enjoying a special kind of existence, and as such it exerts a normative influence on its objectifications. It is true that the realm of possibility is a tightly interlocking field of possibilities that gradually shade off from one another. One might, then, be inclined to argue that the proposition which is a work of art is not clearly demarcated from its neighbors and that one performance is as adequate an objectification of the work of art as another. This observation about the realm of possibility is accurate, but it is irrelevant for the following reason. Looked at from the point of view of art, the realm of possibility is not a flat field, but a plain dotted with hillocks. A work of art is not merely a proposition, it is a proposition capable of exerting a unique sort of attraction. At this point I anticipate and hence merely adumbrate the doctrines of Chapter 7. The unique kind of attraction exerted by an art object concerns the subjective aim of prehensions of it. The art object is an object intended by its maker, through its propositional character, to serve as a lure which will determine the subjective aim of prehensions of it. That subjective aim becomes: to re-create in that process of self-creation, in that concrescing experience, the proposition which is objectified in the prehended performance. Aesthetic experience is hence the experience of aesthetic re-creation. These notions will be elaborated in the next chapter. The point to be made at the moment is that not all of the tightly interlocking possibilities have this power of generating aesthetic re-creation. Those that do stand out as hillocks on the flat field of possibilities.

The theory of hillocks depends in part on the theory of beauty elaborated in Chapter 5, which is that beauty is an eternal object of the subjective species ingressing into the subjective form of certain prehensions. Actualities as well as the objectifications of art objects can encourage the ingression of the eternal object, beauty. The point here is that beauty invites attention to its object. A performance that is experienced as beautiful, qua the beauty attributed to it, encourages the involvement of subjective aim, which is the *sine qua non* of aesthetic experience. It is to be noted that this account does not eliminate the possibility that "the ugly" can be experienced aesthetically; it can because horror, for example, can fascinate and induce aesthetic re-creation.

An example will help clarify these points. The painting hanging before me expresses a proposition about the lonely quietness of a deserted quay in the early morning. If any of the three harmoniously spaced boats were shifted slightly closer to either of the others the unity of the composition would be damaged and the canvas would lose much beauty, i.e. prehensions of it in the mode of causal efficacy would not exhibit beauty as an eternal object ingredient in their subjective forms. Consequently it would fail to attract the kind of attention required for aesthetic re-creation and the painting would lose much of its value—it would fall between hillocks. If, on the other hand, the boats were completely rearranged in a manner even more beautiful than at present, the objectified proposition would be pushed even higher up its hillock. More profoundly, if the stark loneliness of the empty sheds had not been caught by the artist so well, nor the calm shimmer of the water, the proposition itself would be one to which viewers would remain aesthetically indifferent, i.e. it would again fall between hillocks.

The reason for introducing the hillock metaphor is to emphasize that performers recognize that the set of rules for objectification set down by an artist points toward a hillock distinct from the possibilities closely packed around it which is a norm guiding their objectifications. For example, in each acting generation there is a Hamlet who is recognized as standing above his fellow thespians; his objectifications hit their mark. Fritz Kreisler developed a cadenza for the Beethoven Violin Concerto that is recognized as being so apt for the composition that even such a talented performer as Zino Franscescatti acquiesces in its use. I remember once hearing a critic say after a performance of the "Claire de Lune" which was very, very slow in the opening and closing sections and fairly flew through the middle arpeggios: "I'm not sure just what I did hear, but it certainly wasn't Debussy." I agreed with him; a proposition was objectified that evening, but it was not that proposition which is Debussy's "Claire de Lune," and not a proposition of any great aesthetic value.

I shall offer two items from my own experience in an effort to clarify further the relationships between artists and performers on the one hand, and propositions and objectifications on the other. The first item involves an experience I had some time ago as a member of a drama group cast in a one-act play by William Saroyan titled *The Hungerers*. This is an unusual play, replete with surrealistic dialogue, characters who die but continue to declaim, and a stagehand who, with one leg dangling over the apron, reads a book, stirring himself occasionally to move a set, a piece of furniture, or a still-muttering corpse. A smooth-running production developed and was subsequently entered in two competitions. The first was judged by the drama critic of a New York newspaper; in his critique the judge was lavish in his praise of the acting and details of production and singled the performance out for the top award. The second competition was judged by a university professor of drama. The same caliber of performance received no award, and in his critique the professor spent but one sentence on it, which in effect said: "Mr. Saroyan did not have the slightest idea what he was trying to say when he wrote this play so one cannot criticize his players for failing to provide an intelligible performance." Ignoring the question as to whether the professor was right in his analysis of Saroyan's play, he was certainly correct in insisting that one cannot evaluate lighting, timing, diction, pace, etc. in a vacuum. These are all techniques for objectifying a proposition; they enhance the proposition they objectify, but they also derive their *raison d'être* from that proposition. If that proposition is weak, flabby, or otherwise aesthetically ineffective, any given performance of the work is bound to be aesthetically unsatisfactory no matter how polished technically.

The second item involves the Yale première of Archibald MacLeish's *J.B.* I attended this performance in the company of a third-year directing student at the Yale Drama School. This student was convinced that *J.B.* is not good theater, on the grounds that MacLeish had not been successful in making J.B. and his family real, live people with whom the audience could identify itself. I maintained, against him, that if performed with older, more mature actors, in the roles of J.B. and Zeus particularly, this blemish—present obviously enough in the Yale performance—would be seen not to be a weakness of the play itself. The proposition, which *is* the play I maintain, revealed itself through the performance as transcending the performance. My friend has since seen the Broadway production and has granted that Pat Hingle and Christopher Plummer have succeeded in drawing the audience into the drama, i.e. as I would want to say, their performance is a more adequate objectification of the proposition which is *J.B.* than was the Yale production.

The case of *J.B.* will also illustrate another facet of the relationship between propositions and their objectifications. When performed at Yale the proposition *J.B.*, as apart from its objectification, was not right at the very top of its "hillock," to use the previous metaphor. It was, rather, well up the side of a hillock, but nevertheless situated somewhat lower than the crown. The various early objectifications revealed certain less than optimum characteristics of the original *J.B.*, and by the time of the Broadway opening MacLeish had been prevailed upon to alter his original proposition somewhat. For example, it was reported to me that the climactic "blow on the coal of the heart" lines, originally spoken by J.B.'s wife, had been given to J.B. himself, providing a much stronger denouement. This is, of course, nothing unusual; the normal pilgrimage of plays and musicals from Boston to New Haven to Philadelphia before their New York openings is the occasion for much frantic effort not only to perfect techniques for objectification but also to modify the original proposition and push it further up its hillock.

This hillock metaphor I have been using is certainly not elegant, but it contains important insights which will now be elaborated somewhat. Since the metaphor is used to distinguish aesthetically important propositions from aesthetically irrelevant propositions, the relationship between the propositions which are works of art and the propositions which concern logicians is of interest.

Whitehead insists that

> the ordinary logical account of 'propositions' expresses only a restricted aspect of their rôle in the universe,

namely, when they are the data of feelings whose subjective forms are those of judgments. It is an essential doctrine in the philosophy of organism that the primary function of a proposition is to be relevant as a lure for feeling. For example, some propositions are the data of feelings with subjective forms such as to constitute those feelings to be the enjoyment of a joke. Other propositions are felt with feelings whose subjective forms are horror, disgust, or indignation. [PR 37]

He also deplores in strong language the tendency of logicians to ignore all but the narrow class of propositions which interest them directly:

The fact that propositions were first considered in connection with logic, and the moralistic preference for true propositions, have obscured the rôle of propositions in the actual world. Logicians only discuss the judgment of propositions. . . . The result is that false propositions have fared badly, thrown into the dustheap, neglected. But in the real world it is more important that a proposition be interesting than that it be true. The importance of truth is, that it adds to interest. . . . It is, further, to be noticed that the form of words in which propositions are framed also includes an incitement to the origination of an affirmative judgment-feeling. In imaginative literature, this incitement is inhibited by the general context, and even by the form and make-up of the material book. Sometimes there is even a form of words designed to inhibit the formation of a judgment-feeling, such as 'once upon a time.' [PR 395–97]

These passages initially suggested to me the ideas which have since grown and expanded into the present theory. There are propositions which transcend the narrow inter-

ests of logicians. Some of these ultralogical propositions
are works of art and share with those that interest the
logician the ontological status of propositions—here the
Crocean insight into the nature of the art object is pre-
served. But these propositions which are works of art are
propositions exhibiting the primary propositional function
of being lures for feeling. And specifically, they are lures
for a special kind of feeling, aesthetic feeling, i.e. they lure
contemplators into prehending them with the subjective
aim of re-creating them—they seduce subjective aim. This
point will be the basis for the sense in which I admit, in
Chapter 10, to a limited theory of Art for Art's Sake, and
will also emerge more clearly in the discussion of aesthetic
experience in Chapter 7.

The theory embodied in the hillock metaphor also has
important ramifications for the question of the so-called
"immortality" of art, or "inexhaustibility" of art. An art
object is a proposition with the power of seducing subjective aim. Propositions which are art objects are hillocks
which dot the plain of possibility; by saying that a proposition sits on the crown of a hillock I mean that it exerts
commanding control over an overpowering percentage of
subjective aims that encounter it. There are large and
small hillocks, and propositions on the slopes of hillocks
as well as on the crowns of hillocks. The relevance of the
doctrine of "inexhaustibility" to the hillocks metaphor is
just this: the hillocks that dot the plain of potentiality are
in constant flux. They erode away; new hillocks push their
way up from the plain. To interpret this aspect of the metaphor is to point out that propositions which in one climate
of experience are irresistible lures, may be, in another, absolute bores. Theodore L. Shaw, in a series of articles in
a small but lively pamphlet titled *Critical*,[18] has empha-

18. At this writing four issues of *Critical* (Stuart Publications, Boston),
have appeared, each devoted to an article by Shaw. The issues appeared in
October and November 1959 and January and April 1960.

sized the crucial role played in aesthetic experience by "fatigue." In castigating the critics' meaningless use of phrases such as "immorality of art," he opines that every art work "is continually in a process of closer and closer approach to the status of the Wright brothers' airplane, to which we give a place of honor in the Smithsonian Institute, as a tribute to an amazing human achievement, but would not care to fly in, since the sensation of flying may be so much more richly (and safely) sensed in an airplane of the present day." But, he continues,

> the regarding of an art work as inevitably destined to achieve this status does not require that your admiration for it be abandoned. The admiration simply transmutes itself gradually from the fervid admiration you may have felt when the art work's potential for delighting you was still strong and frequent, into a more intellectual and reverential admiration when the art work has become as much as ninety per cent, say, nothing but an exploit. Under such conditions only the most unlikely turn of events can again give it importance as an aesthetic experience.[19]

Shaw's constructive point, which tends to be lost in lusty salvos directed at current art criticism, is that the element of obtrusiveness in an art work which makes it great, which makes it an effective lure for feeling in my terminology, is the very element which weakens its resistance to reiteration, i.e. increases its vulnerability to fatigue.[20] Hence there are levels of erosion on the plain of propositions: cultural advances may impair the power of a proposition to be a lure for feeling, or a given person's resistance to reiteration may wear thin through exposure, and then fatigue will destroy for him the power of certain propositions to lure feeling. This latter case is in keeping with the obvious

19. Ibid. (October 1959), p. 5.
20. Ibid. (November 1959), p. 8.

fact that one does not find an "immortal," "inexhaustible" novel and then read and reread it perpetually; rather one seeks to keep alive the freshness of total aesthetic involvement by roaming ever wider and wider afield in the byways of art.

There is an analogy to this erosion in the class of propositions that concern the logician; a change in situation can change the value of the logician's propositions also. The proposition expressed in the sentence "Eisenhower is President of the United States" did not have the same truth value in December of 1960 as it had in February of 1961. Likewise, the aesthetic value of the propositions which are works of art changes.

Because the hillocks rise and erode, it is impossible to specify the boundaries of art in a rigid way, i.e. to specify those kinds of propositions which exhaust the domain of art. John Myhill has made this point in an interesting manner by arguing away from Gödel's incompleteness theorem and Church's proof that quantification theory admits of no decision procedure.[21] He concludes, "The analogue of Gödel's theorem for aesthetics would therefore be: there is no school of art which permits the production of all beauty and excludes the production of all ugliness. And the analogue of Church's theorem, a weaker statement of course, would run: there is no token (as pleasure or the like) by which you shall know the beautiful when you see it." [22] The analogue of Church's theorem is equivalent to the point I have been making: there is no way of describing those propositions which are works of art such that just some propositions qualify and all others are excluded, i.e. there is no way of specifying beforehand what characteristics a proposition must have in order to lure feeling. Morris Weitz has insisted on the same point:

21. "Some Philosophical Implications of Mathematical Logic," *Review of Metaphysics*, 6 (1952), 165–98.
22. Ibid., pp. 191–92.

"Art," itself, is an open concept. New conditions (cases) have constantly arisen and will undoubtedly constantly arise; new art forms, new movements will emerge, which will demand decisions on the part of those interested, usually professional critics, as to whether the concept should be extended or not. Aestheticians may lay down similarity conditions but never necessary and sufficient ones for the correct application of the concept. . . . What I am arguing, then, is that the very expansive, adventurous character of art, its ever-present changes and novel creations, makes it logically impossible to ensure any set of defining properties.[23]

I agree with Weitz. In suggesting that aesthetic objects have the ontological status of Whiteheadian propositions I am not defining "Art"—I am, rather, proposing what Weitz terms "similarity conditions." Necessary and sufficient conditions are, as Myhill argues, unobtainable, and this is reflected in my theory by the fact that no precise statement can be made of exactly what sorts of propositions can and what sorts can't exert aesthetic lure for feeling.

This examination of the hillock metaphor has been somewhat of a digression; these matters will receive further attention in the subsequent chapter, dealing with aesthetic experience, and in Chapter 9, where the question of truth in art is considered. Having so far developed the theory that works of art are Whiteheadian propositions as it applies to the performer arts, I will turn now to architecture and the two nonperformer arts, painting and sculpture, with the aim of showing how my categories are applicable to these arts.

23. "The Role of Theory in Aesthetics," *Journal of Aesthetics and Art Criticism*, 15 (1956), 32. This article is reprinted in *Problems in Aesthetics*, ed. Morris Weitz.

Architecture and the Nonperformer Arts

Architecture shares the basic characteristic of the performer arts; in this art there is a "language" capable of framing rules or instructions for the objectification of propositions. There has been much talk lately about designing dwellings suitable for elderly people. An architect in New York City might design a system of row-houses to meet this need, make up a set of blueprints, and sell them to a west coast builder, who would follow instructions in objectifying the architect's original vision. As the composer may recognize his partnership with the performer and provide him with a cadenza, so the architect may leave alternatives in, say, construction materials, open to the discretion of the builder: a set of the row-houses in Chicago may be finished with aluminum siding while a set in Philadelphia may be finished with regular clapboards.

A different dimension of architecture appears when one considers a man like Frank Lloyd Wright—a dimension that begins to resemble those of the nonperformer arts. Wright's *Robie House* in Chicago and *Falling Water* at Bear Run, Pennsylvania, though in principle as "performable" as *Hamlet*, have never to my knowledge been objectified but in those instances. This is a characteristic of the nonperformer arts. Another characteristic is that no outside performer stands between the painter's and sculptor's vision and its objectification. The Dessau Bauhaus movement guided by Walter Gropius merged industrial design and construction with architecture in such a way that the architect-designer-artisan is, like the painter or sculptor, artist and performer at one and the same time.[24] As an artist-engineer, the modern architect thinks in terms

24. See Alexander Dorner, *The Way beyond "Art"* (New York, New York University, 1958), passim, for references to the significance of the Bauhaus movement for modern art theory.

of new applications of mathematics,[25] science, and materials much as a Jackson Pollock thinks in terms of new ways to use the conventional materials of painting.

Turning now to the nonperformer arts themselves, to painting and sculpture, the point to be made is that it is intelligible and useful to distinguish the proposition from its objectification in these arts. My position is that the portrait or statue viewed in a gallery is an objectified proposition. The proposition which is the painting, like the proposition which is a musical composition, has a continuous propositional existence which is independent of its objectification. This is not to say that the objectification does not play a role in the artist's discovery of his proposition. In the performer art, music, it is possible that a composer may only succeed in isolating the proposition which is the art object by experimenting on a piano. Likewise, it is possible that a painter may only isolate the proposition he seeks to objectify while working on a canvas. A better parallel with music could be made by referring to the "rides" taken by jazzmen. A jazz classic, e.g. "When the Saints Go Marching In," merely provides a sequence of chords for the soloist to work with plus a melodic line that is simply a guide for weaving those chords together. When a Louis Armstrong goes to work on these raw materials the result is an objectification of a proposition that is only articulated, or isolated, in the act of objectification. There is only one proposition which is a given Wolf *Lied*, but jazz improvization is such that there are as many "Saints" as there are Armstrongs and Biederbeckes to discover new propositions through their objectifications. Painting and

25. The Spanish architect-engineer Eduardo Torroja y Miret explains that, at his own Technical Institute of Construction and Cement, the "sickle-shaped ribs of the pergola that spring from the outside wall and curve elegantly overhead like jets of water frozen in a high wind" are actually "Bernoullian lemniscates with zero end curvature." Quotes from *Time*, 73 (June 1, 1959), 70.

sculpture resemble jazz in this respect; there is, for example, one general structure which is the female form, as there is one general structure underlying "The Saints," but each objectification in stone or in paint of this general form isolates a proposition. Of course Armstrong can be working out in his head during an intermission the ride he intends to take when he climbs back on the bandstand, and a sculptor can work out "in his mind's eye" [26] the general lines of his next statue. Friends connected with a marble quarry in Proctor, Vermont, have described to me how artists prowl about in the company stock yards, and even descend into the quarries, looking for the exact block that will objectify externally a proposition apparently already articulated in the conceived medium of the imagination.

But there are also parallels in the nonperformer arts with the Wolf *Lieder* type of music. It is not uncommon for painters to produce several canvases very similar to one another in an effort to capture the proposition they all embody ever more perfectly—i.e. to push the proposition ever higher on its hillock. A good example would be the London (National Gallery) and Paris (Louvre) versions of Leonardo da Vinci's "Madonna of the Rocks." Leonardo had a vision which he desired to objectify and which he tried to capture more than once. Artists very frequently make numerous preliminary drawings and sketches for their projected objectifications; D. C. Rich has published a whole book (titled *Seurat and the Evolution of "La Grande Jatte"* [27]) dealing with preparations for a single objectification.

A final difference between the performer and nonperformer arts concerns the nature of their objectifications.

26. These matters will be considered again below, Chap. 8, in connection with artistic creation, and I shall there introduce a phrase borrowed from John Hospers to describe this situation—"the conceived medium."

27. Chicago, University of Chicago Press, 1935.

In the performer arts an objectification is a discursive entity that requires the passage of time for its performance and then fades from actuality into objective immortality, while in architecture and the nonperformer arts an objectification, once secured, is an enduring object indifferent to time. The distinction is parallel to that traditionally made between the temporal and the nontemporal arts. It is interesting, however, to note a sense in which the arts within each category approximate to those within the other. For example, in viewing a painting, statue, or cathedral there is an arrangement in the object that compels the eye to move in a certain sequence analogous to the sequence in a musical performance. Also, from the opposite point of view, the allegation sometimes made that Mozart remarked that he could hear a symphony complete in his head in the flash of an instant, exemplifies, whether historically accurate or not, the important truth that the temporal arts demand a familiarity on the part of the contemplator which permits him to gather the discursiveness of the performance into a unity of presence parallel to that which predominates in the nontemporal arts. I suggest that the discursiveness of the temporal arts must be overcome before the objectified proposition can be fully grasped, whereas in the nontemporal arts there must be an appreciation of sequence if the objectified proposition is to register its impact. The basic aesthetic tension of unity within contrast is exemplified here; the arts within each category must approximate to those within the other if this unifying contrast productive of aesthetic experience is to be possible. Music has contrast built into it, hence the composer struggles for unity; architecture has unity built into it, hence the architect struggles for contrasts.

As the temporal and nontemporal arts bend each toward the other, so also the distinction between objectifications

in the performer arts and nonperformer arts, including for
the moment architecture, is not sharp and rigid. The objectifications of the performer arts are in one sense ephemeral, but as objectively immortal, a performance can linger
on in the memory of those who witnessed it. It can even
live in the experience of succeeding generations—as, for
example, the performances of Caruso live in my generation
as a result of descriptions of his powers passed on by those
who heard him in his prime. On the other hand, the Par-
thenon has crumbled and decayed, Joseph Turner's famous
sunsets are losing their brilliance, and the lava layers of
Italy and Greece are strewn with the remnants of great
statuary.

This chapter has introduced a central doctrine of the
aesthetic theory here being presented: that the work of
art has the ontological status of a Whiteheadian proposition. Forster has indicated that works of art "have something general about them," and I suggest that it is their
propositional character. A proposition is not completely
general. By way of contrast, the conceptual feeling of an
eternal object is perfectly general in the sense that no
reference is made to any particular realization of that eternal object (PR 372); Whitehead terms such a feeling an
"unqualified negation." On the other hand, in the physical feeling of a concrete actuality, generality is lost; the
eternal objects involved are immanent, not transcendent.
In the case of a proposition the unqualified generality of a
conceptual feeling is qualified by relevance, but by relevance to a bare logical subject, not to an actuality. The
indefiniteness characteristic of eternal objects is consequently not completely eliminated in a proposition.[28] This

28. See above, p. 65. It is there noted that it is the retention of indefiniteness which serves as a lure for conscious feelings. This is in
keeping with the fact that aesthetic experiences are among the most in-
tensely conscious that we have.

residue of indefiniteness generates the insight that works of art "have something general about them." *Hamlet* is not a play about a particular, concrete man, nor is *J.B.* The characters Hamlet and J.B. are the logical subjects of propositions; hence arises the generality which is ascribed to the works of art which are the propositions which contain them.

I turn now to indicate how this doctrine gives rise to a theory of aesthetic experience as artistic re-creation.

7. Aesthetic Experience

As this book was beginning to take shape, John B. Cobb, Jr., published an article titled "Toward Clarity in Aesthetics." [1] It verified, to my mind, the significance of the ideas I was in the process of developing. Cobb's general presupposition is identical with my own: he holds that, given the present stage of development of scientific psychology, clarity and precision in aesthetic discourse can be achieved only when the central concepts involved are firmly grounded in a speculative philosophy. He selects the epistemology of Whitehead as a tool for determining "what 'the aesthetic' is as the defining and delimiting characteristic of objects felt to be aesthetic . . ." [2]

Cobb's analysis touches upon only a small portion of the ground covered in this book. He tries to state precisely what it means to say that an object is aesthetic and precisely what it means to say that an experience is aesthetic. His analysis is interesting and subtle and has been extremely helpful to me in investigating the same topics. I do feel, however, that his theories are only the tentative conclusions of pioneering research, and the present chapter modifies his doctrine radically. I not only stand on his shoulders in regard to these particular topics, but am building also upon the foundation laid in Chapter 6, a

1. *Philosophy and Phenomenological Research*, 18 (1957), 169–89.
2. Ibid., p. 169.

foundation that presents the problems in a slightly different manner. Though the theory of this chapter will consequently advance beyond his position in significant ways, I shall begin by summarizing briefly the central ideas of his article, which provide the initial distinctions from which I can advance to further considerations. As indicated above, Cobb presents a theory of the aesthetic object as well as of aesthetic experience. In what follows, therefore, the subject matter of Chapter 6 will be a topic of discussion again. I shall argue that Cobb's theory of "the aesthetic" is fruitful primarily in that it points toward an acceptable doctrine of aesthetic experience. His theory fails as an account of "the aesthetic" as a property of objects. I believe my own doctrine of Chapter 6 is capable of performing the role assigned by Cobb to the notion of "the aesthetic." The primary emphasis, however, will be placed on modifying Cobb's insights, in order to present aesthetic experience as aesthetic re-creation.

1. COBB'S THEORY

Cobb begins by making explicit two assumptions supporting his inquiry: "One is that there is a range of objects generally recognized as being of special aesthetic interest. The other is that these objects have in common some distinguishing trait." [3] His purpose is to discover this trait: to determine such a trait, he argues, would be to determine "the aesthetic" as the defining and delimiting characteristic of objects felt to be aesthetic—of objects such as poems, paintings, music, and sculpture generally recognized as being of special aesthetic interest.

After a succinct summary of relevant Whiteheadian categories, Cobb concludes that since whatever is actual has its being in actual occasions (an implicit reference to the ontological principle), "the aesthetic" must be sought

3. Ibid.

(1) in a distinctive form or pattern displayed by individual actual occasions; (2) in a form or pattern displayed by societies of actual occasions; (3) in the relationship of occasions, societies of occasions, or elements within occasions; or (4) in some element within an occasion considered in itself.[4]

The first three alternatives are dismissed as irrelevant to the search for "the aesthetic." Since it is to some element within an occasion considered in itself that the search is now directed, "the aesthetic" must inhere either in the subjective aim of an actual occasion or in some component of prehensions, i.e. initial datum, objective datum, or subjective form. Again the first three are rejected leaving subjective form as the locus of "the aesthetic"; "the distinction between 'the aesthetic' and 'the non-aesthetic' must be made at the level of the subjective forms of prehensions." [5]

One further Whiteheadian distinction is made—between prehensions in the mode of causal efficacy and perceptions in the mode of presentational immediacy—and Cobb is ready to present his theory. Since the subjective form of perception in the mode of presentational immediacy is less determined by the object than is that in the mode of causal efficacy (insofar as the former is determined by the object, it is mediated by the latter), and since " 'the aesthetic' as a property *of the object* must be found in that part of the experience of the prehending human occasion which is determined by the object . . ." [6] it follows that " 'the aesthetic' as a property of objects is to be found initially in the subjective form of prehensions of them in the mode of causal efficacy." [7]

4. Ibid., p. 172.
5. Ibid., p. 175.
6. Ibid., p. 176.
7. Ibid.

In a succinct sentence Cobb characterizes both the object as aesthetic and experience as aesthetic: "To summarize, an object is aesthetic to whatever extent the subjective form of the prehension of it in the mode of causal efficacy is aesthetic; an experience is aesthetic to whatever extent the aesthetic object is determinative of the subjective form of the entire experience." [8] The theory culminates in the following conclusions:

> Art objects are here defined as those which are intended to possess positive aesthetic value or beauty. That is, they are those objects the creators of which strive for such internal relationship of parts as will be prehended as aesthetically satisfactory in the mode of causal efficacy. . . .
>
> The conclusion now reached is that the property shared by aesthetic fields and absent in those which are not thought of as aesthetic is that of yielding or striving to yield an experience of lasting satisfaction in the form or pattern of prehensions in the mode of causal efficacy.[9]

Cobb is quick to note that this analysis does not prescribe the sort of form or pattern that is essential to aesthetic experience; this is, rather, an empirical question. The critic must "feel" in the mode of causal efficacy to see if a given form results in lasting satisfaction. Universal notions such as "complex variety" retain their universality only by sacrificing specificity so that "unity in diversity" can mean little more than "satisfactory form," and is hence unilluminating. Likewise, aesthetic harmony and balance are not identical with mathematical harmony or balance; hence "the question as to what constitutes aesthetic unity, diversity, harmony, balance, and contrast must be answered by ref-

8. Ibid., p. 177.
9. Ibid., p. 179.

erence to the fundamental subjective sense of what is aesthetically satisfactory, rather than being the independent
basis of determining whether or not an object or experience has aesthetic value." [10] Direct experience of satisfaction in the mode of causal efficacy is, then, the criteria
of "the aesthetic" for Cobb. "The aesthetic" considered
as a property of objects is simply that which "causes their
form to be prehend[ed] as satisfactory in the mode of
causal efficacy." [11]

These are the central points in Cobb's exposition. Interesting as his ideas are, as presented they do not constitute an acceptable theory.

II. WEAKNESSES OF COBB'S THEORY

Cobb has been concerned to distinguish his position
from that of Eliseo Vivas, who writes: "an esthetic object
is an object—any object—grasped in such a way as to
give rise to an esthetic experience." [12] Cobb wants to believe that he is being very cool toward the suggestion that
"a certain attitude voluntarily taken is aesthetic, that any
object toward which this attitude is taken is thereby constituted an aesthetic object, and that the entire experience
of the object is indiscriminably an aesthetic experience." [13]
On this issue he also dismisses the theory of Curt John
Ducasse. He quotes Ducasse: "any feeling whatever which
is obtained in aesthetic contemplation, is aesthetic feeling." [14] Of this position Cobb writes:

10. Ibid., p. 180. I might add that Whitehead writes (AI 336): "Now
Harmony is more than logical compatibility, and Discord is more than
logical incompatibility. Logicians are not called in to advise artists."

11. Cobb, p. 181.

12. "A Definition of the Esthetic Experience," *Journal of Philosophy*,
34 (1937), 630, quoted by Cobb, p. 174, n. 5. This article is also reprinted in Eliseo Vivas and Murray Kreiger, *The Problems of Aesthetics*
(New York, Rinehart, 1953), pp. 406–11.

13. Cobb, p. 174.

14. Curt John Ducasse, *The Philosophy of Art* (New York, Lincoln

Ducasse aprently [apparently] holds that every object is intrinsically equally aesthetic and that aesthetic objects vary aesthetically only according to the pleasure or pain of their contemplation . . . The taking of the aesthetic attitude toward objects appears to be a purely voluntary act, determined, that is, by the person rather than by any characteristic of the object. Presumably one is not affected by beauty or ugliness until he has adopted this attitude. My view is that we are constantly affected by aesthetic properties of objects although their influence is most complete and consciously experienced only when we adopt the appropriate attitude. Furthermore, our adopting of that attitude is determined just as much by the intensity of the already existing effect of the object upon us as by our decision to adopt it. Thus "the aesthetic" cannot be defined in complete dependence upon the attitude as Ducasse defines it.[15]

The point I wish to make now is that Cobb's own theory does not serve to advance him beyond the subjectivism of Ducasse and Vivas, much as he wants it to.

Cobb's overriding concern is to show that "the aesthetic" is a property of objects. A key passage, quoted above, is the following: " 'the aesthetic' as a property of objects is to be found initially in the subjective form of prehensions of them in the mode of causal efficacy." [16] This is a crucial passage for Cobb but at the same time a very strange one. The word "initially" here can mean two things, and on either rendering the theory falls to the ground.

First, the word may mean that "the aesthetic" is not

Mac Veagh, Dial Press, 1929), p. 189, quoted by Cobb, p. 174, n. 5. Relevant passages of this book are reprinted in Vivas and Kreiger, pp. 358–76.
15. Cobb, p. 174, n. 5.
16. Ibid., p. 176.

originally found in the objects at all, but that it first emerges in the subjective forms of prehensions of the objects in the mode of causal efficacy and then is somehow transferred to the object as a property of the object. This interpretation will never stand up in the light of the Whiteheadian metaphysics. An object is "objectivé," i.e. it is objectively immortal and as such just what it is through all time. Whitehead writes: "Actual entities perish, but do not change; they are what they are" (PR 52). Again, "the final 'satisfaction' of an actual entity is intolerant of any addition" (PR 71). These quotes are cited by Christian [17] who himself writes:

> The satisfaction of an actual occasion, when it has lost its immediacy, is not only objective but also immortal. The satisfied occasion persists and retains its identity as an object throughout its adventures in the future. The satisfaction is "fully determinate . . . as to its objective character for the transcendent creativity" (PR 38).[18]

If the objective character of an object is fully determinate, it is impossible for a property of objects to be found originally in the subjective forms of entities which must necessarily be subsequent to those objects since they prehend them. Hence if "the aesthetic" is a property of objects, it cannot be found initially in the subjective forms of prehensions of them in this first sense.

But secondly, the word "initially" may mean that "the aesthetic" is discovered initially in subjective forms though originally located in the object as a property of the object. But this interpretation also creates difficulties for Cobb. He wants to hold, as indicated above, that his analysis does not prescribe the sort of form or pattern that is essential

17. *Whitehead's Metaphysics*, pp. 34–35.
18. Ibid., p. 38.

to aesthetic experience; this remains an empirical question. The question of what constitutes aesthetic unity, diversity, harmony, and balance must be answered by reference to the fundamental subjective sense of what is aesthetically satisfactory, he insists. But now he is really no better off than either Vivas or Ducasse. There is nothing in Cobb to permit him to say that what is aesthetic in the subjective form of one prehender will be aesthetic in that of another, or even that what strikes one prehender as aesthetic today will so strike him tomorrow. Cobb wishes to say that that in objects which "causes their form to be prehend[ed] as satisfactory in the mode of causal efficacy" [19] is "the aesthetic" and that it is a property of objects. But his position cannot preclude the possibility that one property might make A prehend object X as aesthetic today and another property might make A prehend X as aesthetic tomorrow. But to say that a given, fixed property of X is aesthetic one moment and not the next is to preclude the possibility of referring to "the aesthetic" as a *property of objects* in view of Whitehead's dictum, quoted above, that the entity "objectivé" is intolerant of any alteration. What Cobb can assert is that *something* in an object is required to touch off a feeling of satisfaction in a subjective form, though it may be now this, now that property of the object which causes the aesthetic satisfaction. Cobb asserts that in the theory of Ducasse, "The taking of the aesthetic attitude toward objects appears to be a purely voluntary act, determined, that is, by the person rather than by any characteristic of the object." [20] Now surely on Ducasse's theory *some* characteristic of the object is relevant as producing pleasure in that act of contemplation, and I fail to see how Cobb's theory differs in any respect from Ducasse's doctrine. Cobb's effort to pre-

19. Cobb, p. 181.
20. Ibid., p. 174, n. 5.

sent an objective theory of "the aesthetic" has fallen short of the mark.

It will be recalled that Cobb initially assumed [21] that objects generally recognized as being of special aesthetic interest have in common some distinguishing trait. He further argued that to determine such a trait would be to determine "the aesthetic" as the defining and delimiting characteristic of objects felt to be aesthetic. In Chapter 6 [22] I argued, citing John Myhill and Morris Weitz for support, that a set of defining properties for "Art" cannot be specified. My own theory that works of art are propositions was advanced as a "similarity condition," not a necessary and sufficient condition, since, obviously, there are propositions which are not art objects. Hence I can agree with Cobb that objects generally recognized as being of special aesthetic interest have in common some distinguishing trait. But such a trait cannot be a defining characteristic. Therefore it is really no surprise to discover that Cobb's attempt to enunciate such a defining characteristic is internally inconsistent.

Cobb wished "the aesthetic" to be a defining property and a property of the object. I have shown that as he wished to conceive of "the aesthetic," it cannot be a property of the object. The similarity condition of art objects which I have emphasized is their propositional character, and this *is* an objective property of the art object.

III. The Present Theory of Aesthetic Experience

Cobb himself takes a few tentative steps along the path here to be laid out. He notes that even though "the aesthetic" is initially located in the subjective form of prehensions in the mode of causal efficacy, "its importance

21. See above, p. 135.
22. See above, pp. 126–27.

rests to a great extent upon its potentiality for the determination of the total occasion of experience and especially
of the perception in the mode of presentational immediacy." [23] He notes that only when an art object

> is contemplated for its own sake or for the sake of that
> which it effects in the experience of the contemplator
> can it-make its full aesthetic impact. When this occurs
> the process of transmutation into the mode of presen-
> tational immediacy is governed more or less completely
> by the datum of the prehension rather than by a prac-
> tical subjective aim. In this case the subjective aim is
> that the entire occasion be maximally determined by
> the art object.[24]

These suggestions contain the seed of the doctrine now
to be presented.

It is my contention that an experience is aesthetic when
it is experience of an objectified proposition which lures
the subjective *aim* of that occasion of experience into re-
creating in its own process of self-creation the proposition
objectified in the prehended performance. A reconsideration of Whitehead's account of subjective aim will clarify
this doctrine. Whitehead writes: "The 'subjective aim,'
which controls the becoming of a subject, is that subject
feeling a proposition with the subjective form of purpose
to realize it in that process of self-creation" (PR 37). Normally this proposition is the vision of what that subject
might become; it is a vision of the potentialities relevant
to its concrescence as they are prehended in the hybrid
physical prehension of God. I am suggesting that in aesthetic experience the normal goals and aims of everyday
living are suspended; in grasping the subjective aim of one
who experiences it aesthetically, the art object insists that

23. Cobb, p. 177.
24. Ibid.

it be experienced as an end in itself. It temporarily short-circuits the long-range, overarching subjective aims that shape life patterns and dominate ordinary living. These notions will be developed more fully in Chapter 7. At the moment I insist that aesthetic experience transports the experiencer into the "world of art" simply because when an art object objectified by a performance is *aesthetically* prehended, *this objectified proposition is the datum for the subjective aim of that experience.* The subjective *aim* of such an aesthetic experience is *to re-create in that process of self-creation, in that concrescing experience, the proposition which is objectified in the prehended performance.*

It will be recalled that Forster insists that great literature "transforms the man who reads it towards the condition of the man who wrote, and brings to birth in us also the creative impulse." His insight acquires a precise interpretation in terms of this theory.

Aesthetic experience as here defined is the experience of aesthetic re-creation. If the proposition objectified in a performance is not aesthetically re-created by the contemplator, then his experience is not aesthetic. This theory clearly and irrevocably distinguishes itself from the position taken by Vivas, Ducasse, and (I have argued) Cobb. The distinction is that between prehending an *actuality* with a subjective *form* exhibiting the eternal object of the subjective species, beauty, on the one hand, and prehending an *objectified proposition* with the subjective *aim* of re-creating that proposition in that process of self-creation, on the other. Cobb has written that "an object is aesthetic to whatever extent the subjective form of the prehension of it in the mode of causal efficacy is aesthetic . . ." [25] I would modify this doctrine of "the aesthetic" and maintain that an object, any object, be it actuality or proposition, is *beautiful* if the subjective *form* of a prehension

25. Ibid.

of it contains the eternal object of the subjective species, beauty. I shall develop my theory of beauty shortly. But at the moment I wish to distinguish this theory of beauty, which is analogous to Cobb's theory of "the aesthetic" and to the theories of Vivas and Ducasse, from my theory of aesthetic experience. Aesthetic experience is experience of an *objectified proposition* such that the proposition acts as a lure and seduces the subjective *aim* of that occasion of experience into re-creating in its own process of self-creation the proposition objectified in the prehended performance.

IV. AESTHETIC AND NONAESTHETIC ATTENTION

In conjunction with his view that an aesthetic object is any object grasped in such a way as to give rise to an aesthetic experience, Vivas argues that, "An aesthetic experience is an experience of rapt attention which involves the intransitive apprehension of an object's immanent meanings in their full presentational immediacy." [26] Cobb points out, but fails to deal satisfactorily with, the difficulty in this view. He asks:

> If we take the same attitude toward an acrobat which we take toward a drama, does the experience become thereby equally aesthetic? Does an attitude of intransitive attention toward the sounds of the night in a jungle, which arises out of the fascination of novelty, determine the object to be aesthetic in the same degree as attention evoked by the beauty of a great symphony? This difficulty cannot be surmounted by asserting that the more aesthetic object is the one which most facilitates the continuation of the aesthetic attitude of intransitive attention, for we may

26. "A Definition of the Aesthetic Experience," p. 631.

remain spellbound by athletic prowess, by a magician's tricks, or by novel sights and sounds just as readily as by music or painting.[27]

He goes on to comment on the attention theory in a manner relevant to the present doctrine:

> If it is asserted by the proponents of the attention theory that they mean intransitive attention evoked by certain qualities in the object or arising out of certain kinds of interest in it, then the question becomes that of distinguishing aesthetic and non-aesthetic attention in terms of some factor other than attention.[28]

This is a challenge Cobb himself tries to meet in terms of his theory of "the aesthetic" as a property of objects. It has been shown that he fails. I believe my own categories permit the accomplishment of the job Cobb recognizes has to be done.

The identification of aesthetic experience with aesthetic re-creation embodies both an objective and a subjective dimension in the distinction between aesthetic and nonaesthetic attention. Turning first to the objective dimension: the propositional character of art objects is unmistakably an objective property of art objects and also plays an important role in distinguishing between aesthetic and non-aesthetic attention.

As objectified in a sensuous medium by a performance, the art object is still propositional. That this is so is clearly seen by comparing the actuality of the medium with the propositionality of the art work itself. For example, an art dealer examines a canvas to make sure it isn't ripped or

27. Cobb, p. 174.
28. Ibid., pp. 174–75.

hasn't had water dripping on it; his examination is not aesthetic, for he is prehending an actuality, not a proposition. Likewise an art historian, peering through a microscope at some brush strokes in order to learn something about the technique of an artist, is prehending an actuality, not a proposition, and his attention is nonaesthetic. The same is true of the high-fidelity addict trying to synchronize woofer and tweeter. A striking example is that suggested by Edward Bullough and Gertrude Lippincott as I have quoted them in Chapter 6: the lecherous old man in the front row who never gets beyond the ballerina's figure in his prehensions has not experienced the ballet, which is a proposition, but has remained at the level of the actuality of the sensuous performal medium. It is true that he may have been enthralled, spellbound, but this intransitive attention is not aesthetic. He has prehended an *actuality* with the subjective *forms*, say, of delight and desire, but he has missed completely the proposition objectified in the performance and his attention is nonaesthetic. It may be quite correct to say that he prehends the ballerina as being beautiful in this case, for I would maintain that actualities as well as propositions can be prehended with a subjective *form* embodying the eternal object of the subjective species, beauty. The locus of beauty is subjective *form*, hence beauty is a broader notion than aesthetic; to prehend something as beautiful is not necessarily to experience aesthetically, as I shall argue in the next section which deals specifically with beauty.

These comments about ballet emerge more clearly if ballet is contrasted with burlesque. The theory being presented here suggests that burlesque is ballet "stripped" of its propositional character. In a burlesque show the idea is to encourage the patron to focus his attention upon actualities; a fortiori, the attitude of the patron could not possibly be aesthetic. It has been pointed out to me that burlesque shows fairly abound with "propositioning," and it has been suggested that this may vitiate somewhat my last point. In one sense, certainly, "propositions" are made from the runway, but my point would be that at a burlesque house there is complete loss of Distance [29] on the part of the audience because the predicative patterns involved are attributed to actualities *qua* actualities and not to a performal medium *qua* objectifying the logical subject of a proposition. Sophisticated strippers, such as Gypsy Rose Lee in her heyday, or elegantly staged shows such as the "Folies Bergère," represent an interesting mixture; a certain modicum of the propositional element is inserted into the proceedings, with the result that attention is encouraged to shift between an aesthetic and nonaesthetic character in a rather discomforting manner.

It is clear, then, that the propositional character of the art object serves as an objective factor capable of distinguishing aesthetic and nonaesthetic attention.

On the other hand, the identification of aesthetic experience with aesthetic re-creation contains a subjective distinction between aesthetic and nonaesthetic attention, parallel to and integrated with the objective distinction just discussed. The person who prehends an objectified art object need not experience that performance aesthetically. A dim-witted, cauliflower-eared ex-prizefighter might stare hard for a long time at a painting and never experience it aesthetically. Ducasse makes this same point in a footnote rebuttal of Henri Delacroix's claim that there are several varieties of aesthetic contemplation.[30] Ducasse insists that Delacroix's arguments

> seem to me to show only that the response of some
> people to works of art is not aesthetic contemplation

29. See above, p. 109.
30. Delacroix, *Psychologie de l'art* (Paris, Felix Alcan, 1927), pp. 67, 118.

[i.e. is not aesthetic re-creation and hence not aesthetic experience, in my terminology] but something else. For instance, he himself says that the enjoyment derived from reading novels is usually that of giving us the illusion of living through the adventures described. But obviously then, this enjoyment is that of vicarious adventure, which is no more aesthetic than the precisely similar pleasure of watching a football game, a thrilling rescue, or a dramatic escape.[31]

The *aesthetic* contemplation of an art object demands that the contemplator have the ability to seize the proposition objectified by the performance as the datum for subjective aim and then successfully carry out that aim to re-create the proposition in his own experience. Real aesthetic experience, i.e. aesthetic re-creation, requires ability, background, and hard work. Aesthetically sensitive people know better than to try to prehend art objects when they are tired and they know that aesthetic attention cannot be successfully sustained over too considerable periods of time. The present theory provides a rationale for these empirical observations.

Other empirical data followed simply and logically from the subjective side of the present theory, just as the observations above about art historians and ballet follow neatly from the objective aspects of the theory. For example, it provides a rationale for criticism in the arts. Aesthetic re-creation is not guaranteed simply by confrontation with an art object. Dim wits, as in the case of the prizefighter mentioned above, are not the only deterrent to aesthetic experience. In the case of many, if not most, works of art the propositions are involved and complex. A prehender may be alert enough mentally and yet fail to discover the proposition objectified in a performance in

31. Ducasse, *The Philosophy of Art*, p. 138, n. 5.

all its richness and subtle complexity; to him it may seem rather trivial and confused simply because he does not have the historical or critical background required to understand the proposition expressed by the artist. One has to learn the language of art as one has to learn the language of the French; art is an international language only to the extent that people of all nations have learned to understand it. The critic's function is to clarify the subject matter of the proposition expressed in the objectification so that it becomes intelligible to a less sophisticated prehender. Here the New Criticism has a definite role to play. I can recall, for example, the enlightenment gained from the analysis of Eliot's "The Love Song of J. Alfred Prufrock" in Brooks and Warren's classic, *Understanding Poetry*.[32] The art historian also performs this same function, eminently in the case of Erwin Panofsky, for instance.[33]

This theory also provides a metaphysical rationale for the conclusions reached by Vernon Lee in her empirical studies of the psychology of music. Miss Lee distinguishes *listening* to music, *hearing* music, and merely *overhearing* music. "Listening," she reports in summarizing her questionnaires,

> implied the most active attention moving along every detail of composition and performance, taking in all the relations of sequences and combinations of sounds

32. Cleanth Brooks and Robert Penn Warren, *Understanding Poetry* (New York, Henry Holt, revised ed. 1955) pp. 429–44.

33. See his essays collected under the title *Meaning In the Visual Arts*, Garden City, Doubleday, 1955; the chapter titled "Symbolism and Durer's 'Melencolia I'" from his *The Life and Art of Albrecht Durer*, Princeton, Princeton University Press, 1955—reprinted in Morris Weitz, ed., *Problems in Aesthetics*, pp. 360–79; and the essay "The History of Art as a Humanistic Discipline," from T. M. Greene, ed., *The Meaning of the Humanities* (Princeton, Princeton University Press, 1940) and reprinted in Weitz, ed., *Problems in Philosophy*, pp. 288–95.

as regards pitch, intervals, modulations, rhythms and intensities, holding them in the memory and coordinating them in a series of complex wholes, similar (this was an occasional illustration) to that constituted by all the parts, large and small, of a piece of architecture; and these architecturally coordinated groups of sound-relations, i.e. these audible shapes made up of intervals, rhythms, harmonies and accents, themselves constituted the meaning of music to this class of listeners; the meaning in the sense not of a message different from whatever conveyed it, but in the sense of an interest, an importance, residing in the music and inseparable from it.[34]

"Hearing" is not simply an inferior species of this same activity, but "one whose comparative poverty from the musical side is eked out and compensated by other elements."[35] "Hearers" have moments of "listening," but

instead of constituting the bulk of their musical experience (in such a way that any other thought is recognized as irrelevant) these moments of concentrated and active attention to the musical shapes are like islands continually washed over by a shallow tide of other thoughts: memories, associations, suggestions, visual images and emotional states, ebbing and flowing round the more or less clearly emergent musical perceptions, in such a way that each participates of the quality of the other, till they coalesce, forming a homogeneous and special contemplative condition, into whose blend of musical and non-musical thoughts there enters nothing which the "Hearer" can recog-

34. *Music and Its Lovers* (London, George Allen and Unwin, 1932), p. 31.
35. Ibid., p. 32.

nize as inattention, for which, on the contrary, the concentrated musical "Listener" recognizes the lapses and divagations whereof he complains.[36]

Miss Lee stresses, however—an important point for my application of her analysis—that attention to the music itself does play a crucial role in "hearing":

> For these intermittently and imperfectly perceived sequences and combinations of sounds *do* play a very important part in these day-dreams. By their constancy, regularity and difference from anything else, they make and enclose a kind of inner ambiance in which these reveries live their segregated and harmonious life.[37]

The context of Miss Lee's discussion indicates that she might be willing to follow me in the suggestion that "hearing" covers a spectrum which ranges on the one end from an activity close to "listening" and on the other to the point where "hearing" music "lapses into merely *over-hearing* it." [38] I want to suggest that "listening" constitutes aesthetic re-creation and that consequently the "listener" experiences music aesthetically. As the contemplation shifts downward through "hearing" and finally evaporates into "overhearing," so the aesthetic element in the experience dwindles and finally disappears. A summarizing statement in Lee supports this interpretation. She concludes:

> And the first fruits of my Questionnaires have therefore been the establishing of a distinction between listening to music and merely hearing it; between a response to music such as *implies intellectual and aesthetic activity of a very intense, bracing and elevat-*

36. Ibid.
37. Ibid., pp. 32–33.
38. Ibid., p. 31.

ing kind; and a response to music consisting largely of emotional and imaginative day-dreams . . .[39]

The italicized passage is in line with my comments above concerning the effort involved in aesthetic re-creation. Aesthetic re-creation is an activity of a very intense kind; it is the intense activity of re-creating in the immediacy of personal, first person experience the proposition prehended as objectified in a performance. Experiences of "listening" are of this intense, re-creative character and are aesthetic; the higher instances of "hearing," where the "inner ambiance" created by spells of concentrated and active attention to the music is quite considerable, are also aesthetic, though of a weaker intensity. Mere "overhearing" is an instance of nonaesthetic attention.

While admiring Miss Lee's analysis greatly, I would not want to be bound by it in all its details. My comments on Clive Bell and Eduard Hanslick in Chapter 6 [40] show I would argue that her conclusions underestimate the role played by emotion in "listening"; I feel that the *positive* recognition of the dynamic properties of musical movement as being components in definite emotional states is an integral part of "listening." [41] Stephen Pepper has registered an eloquent protest against the overintellectualism lurking in Miss Lee's account.

A certain balance of emotional fusion and analytic discrimination is the normal aesthetic experience. A man who habitually flies off into emotional ecstasy in the presence of a work of art is likely to lack depth of appreciation, even if the emotion is relevant. But it is better to do this than drift into the opposite habit of considering a work of art only in a cold, analytic

39. Ibid., p. 33. My italics.
40. See above, p. 116.
41. See above, p. 114.

way. This hard-boiled attitude is very disconcerting to a novice who is eager to appreciate, and full of potential enthusiasm. The calm technical judgments of a connoisseur, especially when flavored with sarcastic innuendoes about callow ebullitions, is stifling to emotion and the young man becomes afraid to enter into the work he wants to appreciate. He begins insincerely to emulate the manner of the expert, and to imitate his witticisms. Actually, if he but knew it, his natural effusions, thin as they may be, are closer to a realization of the work, than the erudite comments of such an expert.[42]

In support of his view Pepper calls no less a witness than William James, who writes of such a critic whose expertise "has blunted mere emotional excitability as much as it has sharpened taste and judgment":

". . . A sentimental layman would feel, and ought to feel, horrified on being admitted to such a critic's mind to see how cold, how thin, how void of human significance, are the motives for favor and disfavor that there prevail. The capacity to make a nice spot on the wall will outweigh a picture's whole content; a foolish trick of words will preserve a poem; an utterly meaningless fitness of sequence in one musical composition set at naught any amount of 'expressiveness' in another" (Psych. vol. ii, p. 471).[43]

As Pepper concludes, "It is the balance between these opposites that gives real good taste, and makes the genuine expert." [44]

The reason for this digression into Pepper and James is to indicate my sympathy for this aspect of their views

42. *Aesthetic Quality* (New York, Scribner's, 1937), pp. 106–7.
43. Quoted ibid., p. 108.
44. Ibid.

and hence to dissociate myself from any charges of over-intellectualism that might be leveled at Miss Lee. The overarching point, however, which it has been the aim of this section to make, has been sufficiently argued; the present theory is capable of distinguishing aesthetic from non-aesthetic attention.

v. BEAUTY

The theory of beauty which I hold has already been adumbrated. Whitehead speaks of beauty as a "quality" (AI 366–67). Christian notes that though Whitehead refers to beauty as a quality, it is one of a group of qualities that "Whitehead would no doubt call eternal objects . . ." [45] Beauty is an eternal object of the subjective species that ingresses into the subjective form of prehensions. Beauty is a way that things are felt; it is *how* a subject prehends an object. Beauty itself is defined as "the mutual adaptation of the several factors in an occasion of experience" (AI 324). Whitehead makes it clear that this harmonious adaptation relates to subjective form: "the perfection of Beauty is defined as being the perfection of Harmony; and the perfection of Harmony is defined in terms of Subjective Form" (AI 325). Beauty is, then, an eternal object of the subjective species which ingresses into the subjective form of a concrescence when that subjective form exhibits an harmonious adaptation of elements.

The sense in which *objects* are *beautiful* emerges from this theory. Whitehead writes:

> in the analysis of an occasion, some parts of its objective content may be termed Beautiful by reason of their conformal contribution to the perfection of

45. *Whitehead's Metaphysics*, p. 203. See AI 324, where Whitehead writes that "Beauty is a quality which finds its exemplification in actual occasions: or put conversely, it is a quality in which such occasions can severally participate."

the subjective form of the complete occasion. This
secondary sense of the term Beauty is more accurately
to be considered as a definition of the term 'Beautiful.' . . . But in all its senses, 'beautiful' means the
inherent capability for the promotion of Beauty when
functioning as a datum in a percipient occasion. When
'Beauty' is ascribed to any component in a datum, it
is in this secondary sense. [AI 328–29]

When beauty is ascribed to an object in this secondary
sense, it becomes very tempting to conceive of beauty as
Cobb conceives of "the aesthetic," i.e. as an objective property of objects. But Whitehead makes it clear that this
secondary sense of the term "beauty" is subordinate to and
depends upon the first. "The objective content is 'beautiful' by reason of the Beauty that would be realized in that
[concrescing] occasion by a fortunate exercise of its spon-
taneity" (AI 328). Cobb's error was a failure to realize
that this secondary sense of the term "beauty" cannot, in
the Whiteheadian scheme, break away from its dependence upon the primary meaning.

I maintain that not every experience of beauty is an aesthetic experience. I personally find a certain rich shade of
blue very pleasing; I might look at a blue blanket, find
the factors in that experience harmoniously adapted, and
hence be led to say that the blanket is beautiful. But my
experience would not be aesthetic. I have seen abstract
canvases in art galleries that embodied beautiful colors,
but I have had no aesthetic experience in contemplating
them. There has been no way of "getting inside" such
paintings; there are no propositions that can lure one into
"the world they create," for they create no world. Such
canvases can be attractive, pretty, even beautiful, but in
contemplating them one simply encounters an actuality
and searches in vain for their propositional, aesthetic di-

mension. This type of empty, pointless abstract painting is to significant art as burlesque is to ballet.

To do justice to abstract art it should be noted that it does share certain characteristics with music. Like music, abstract art contains a dynamic element of movement, and, as is the case with music, this dynamic element depends upon "you" understood for the logical subject of the proposition objectified in the painting. But abstract art is at a definite disadvantage in comparison to music because the composer has an infinitely more powerful and varied supply of dynamic elements at his command than does the artist. If the artist foregoes the rich supply of logical subjects readily available to him and elects to compete in the realm of the composer, where only the predicative pattern is supplied by the creator, he sets himself a formidable task in attempting to mold dynamic elements out of color and form. It can be done and some abstract art approaches the aesthetic significance of music, but much does not, and degenerates to the aesthetic indifference of burlesque.[46]

The concept of beauty will receive a further development in Chapter 9; now, to conclude this initial discussion of beauty, and this chapter on aesthetic experience, I shall consider briefly the question of natural beauty. Certainly I would hold that blankets, sunsets, and automobiles can be beautiful in the precise sense specified by Whitehead

46. The comparison of abstract art to music has frequently been made, of course. Helen Gardner cites Wassily Kandinsky, "who, with a thorough understanding of the psychological effect of each element, and of the interrelationship of elements, composed paintings devoid of representational content which convey, like music, certain moods or 'soul states' " (*Art Through The Ages*, New York, Harcourt, Brace, 1948, p. 735). Kandinsky is certainly one of the most successful practitioners of nonobjective painting. His own book, *Concerning the Spiritual in Art* (New York, Whittenborn, Schultz, 1947), contains many excellent points which I find easily translatable into my own theory. He continually makes the parallel with music, and it is interesting to note that Kandinsky was also a musician who played the piano and the cello.

in the passages quoted above. But is our experience of a
sunset aesthetic? Aesthetic experience is experience which
is aesthetically re-creative, and aesthetically re-creative experience must not be confused with the passive experience
of beauty. Theodore Greene insists on this distinction.

> We must here distinguish between mere natural mani-
> festation and artistic expression. . . . A work of art
> always expresses in a unique manner an interpreta-
> tion of some subject-matter. It is the expression, *via*
> artistic form, of an intelligible artistic content. . . .
> Is nature in the raw ever expressive as art is expressive?
> It seems indubitable that whatever meaning man may
> be able to discover in nature is not expressed by nature
> itself as the artist's meaning finds expression in his
> art.[47]

My terminology is different from Greene's, but in insisting on the propositional character of art objects I am emphasizing much the same point that he is emphasizing with
his insistence on expression of intelligible artistic content.
Aesthetic experience, for both of us, involves meaning, and
nature itself does not reveal meaning unless it be put there
by the man who encounters nature.[48] This suggests that,

47. *The Arts and the Art of Criticism* (Princeton, Princeton University
Press, 1940), p. 11.
48. Greene notes that man "may also see in natural beauty the expression of a cosmic purpose. The Psalmist is not alone in believing that the
heavens declare the glory of God and that the firmament showeth His
handiwork." But he goes on to add, "If we take the whole of nature as a
unified cosmic process we can, no doubt, believe it to manifest whatever
we conceive ultimate reality to be—a divine providence, or a cosmic principle indifferent to spiritual and moral values, or a satanic impulse to
destruction and decay. But can we reasonably assert that nature as a whole,
and, more specifically, such formal beauty as nature itself manifests, does
unequivocally exhibit any such inner cosmic character? Could the Psalmist
have conceived of the heavens as a declaration of the glory of God had he
not *already* been possessed of an assured religious faith? Did he not merely
find in nature confirmation of an already well-established belief in Divine
Providence?" (pp. 8, 10–11).

rather than being aesthetic experience, the encounter with a sunset, or a mountain range, is a creative experience. Greene writes:

> No natural object or scene is ever bounded by a "frame," i.e., any set limits indicative of where the aesthetic object in question begins and ends. For example, how much should be included in a "sunset," or a "forest glade," or a "mountain peak," if these are to be viewed as aesthetic objects? What are the boundaries of nature's "works of art"? These questions nature herself always leaves unanswered. But if we supply the answer and assume the responsibility of bounding an object of natural beauty, we contribute, by that very act, to whatever beauty may appear within these boundaries. To this extent our response has been creative rather than strictly re-creative.[49]

His point is certainly correct. As we step to one side, changing our perspective, or shade our eyes with a hand, etc., we enhance or detract from the mutual adaptation of the factors in our experience and hence augment or attenuate the ingression of beauty into our experience. As was noted in Chapter 6,[50] beauty invites attention to its object and encourages the involvement of subjective aim. Beauty also increases resistance to reiteration.[51] But as Greene insists, man's "aesthetic reaction to nature resembles that of the painter and the poet rather than that of the critic. It is predominantly an act of artistic creation, not of re-creative discovery." [52] This point leads logically to the next chapter, where the concept of artistic creation will be analyzed in detail.

49. Ibid., p. 9.
50. See above, p. 119.
51. See above, p. 125.
52. Greene, p. 10.

8. Artistic Creation

AESTHETICIANS have sometimes resorted to the notion of
a divine madness in trying to account for the phenomena
of artistic creation. Unless carefully specified, such a notion carries one not the slightest bit further toward a philosophical understanding of artistic creation than does the
"bucket" metaphor of E. M. Forster. Ortega y Gasset
warns: "Better beware of notions like genius and inspiration; they are a sort of magic wand and should be used
sparingly by anyone who wants to see things clearly." [1]
Jacques Maritain states precisely what must be done if
philosophical understanding is to be attained: "I think
that what we have to do is to make the Platonic Muse descend into the soul of man, where she is no longer Muse
but creative intuition; and Platonic inspiration descend
into the intellect united with imagination, where inspiration from above the soul becomes inspiration from above
conceptual reason, that is, poetic experience." [2] It is the
great virtue of Maritain's analysis to have shown how the
standard concepts used in Thomism to describe the structure of the intellect and the normal birth of ideas can be
used to illuminate the process of artistic creation. After
describing these concepts he concludes:

1. "Notes on the Novel," *The Dehumanization of Art and Other Writings on Art and Culture* (Garden City, Doubleday, 1956), p. 54.
2. *Creative Intuition in Art and Poetry* (New York, Meridian Books,
1957), p. 66.

Well, if there is in the spiritual unconscious a non-conceptual or preconceptual activity of the intellect even with regard to the birth of the concepts, we can with greater reason assume that such a nonconceptual activity of the intellect, such a nonrational activity of reason, in the spiritual unconscious, plays an essential part in the genesis of poetry and poetic inspiration. Thus a place is prepared in the highest parts of the soul, in the primeval translucid night where intelligence stirs the images under the light of the Illuminating Intellect, for the separate Muse of Plato to descend into man, and dwell within him, and become a part of our spiritual organism.[3]

Maritain has eloquently described the problem upon which this chapter will center, that of showing how the metaphysical categories of Whitehead's system have prepared a place for the separate Muse of Plato to descend into man. I will show how these categories can be utilized to illuminate the process of artistic creation and will also relate the theory that emerges to the doctrines of Chapters 6 and 7.

I. ULTERIORITY AND TRANSMUTATION

"Stopping by Woods on a Snowy Evening" is one of Robert Frost's best-known poems. An interviewer, upon remarking to Frost that this poem had often been interpreted as a death poem, evoked the mischievous reply, "I never intended that, but I did have the feeling it was loaded with ulteriority." [4] Frost's reply is suggestive and perplexing. Precisely what does it mean to say that a poem is "loaded with ulteriority"? I shall begin this chapter by investigating the notion of "ulteriority" with the help of Whitehead's category of transmutation.

3. Ibid., pp. 73–74.
4. Quoted by Milton Bracker in "The 'Quietly Overwhelming' Robert Frost," *New York Times Magazine* (November 30, 1958), p. 57.

Transmutation was conceived in what might be termed a "vertical" manner in Chapter 3; the function of transmutation was described in terms of the basic problem inhering in any monadic cosmology, the problem of deriving macrocosmic perception from a multiplicity of atomic, or microcosmic entities. I wish to suggest now that Whitehead's theory of experience as "significance" is clarified if this vertical transmutation is supplemented by what I shall term horizontal transmutation. I shall first characterize this horizontal transmutation, showing how it supports the doctrine of experience as significance, and then utilize the notion of horizontal transmutation to explain ulteriority.

Transmutation horizontally conceived is no longer a category to integrate microcosmic entities into macrocosmic perceptions; it is a category to concentrate macrocosmic entities into *one focal point of experience.* This point will emerge more clearly in the light of a passage from Whitehead's early work, *The Principles of Natural Knowledge.*

> What is 'significance'? Evidently this is a fundamental question for the philosophy of natural knowledge, which cannot move a step until it has made up its mind as to what is meant by this 'significance' which is experience.
>
> 'Significance' is the relatedness of things. To say that significance is experience, is to affirm that perceptual knowledge is nothing else than an apprehension of the relatedness of things, namely of things in their relations and as related. [PNK 12]

It is my point that in Whitehead's mature theory, which is a working out of the metaphysical implications of this early doctrine of experience, the notion of horizontal transmutation is essential as it is one of the operations productive of experience as significance. It is needed because even when vertical transmutation has occurred at the second phase of concrescence, the concrescing subject does not yet encounter experience as fully significant. As was made clear in Chapter 3, the comparative feelings at phase III can be either physical purposes or propositional feelings. In the case of a transmuted physical feeling at phase III which is a physical purpose, apprehension of the relatedness of things is at a minimum and hence the significance is small and there is a minimal experience. The full, rich experience of conscious, intelligent creatures is only possible when an apprehension of the relatedness of things is present on a scale adequate to generate momentous significance. Whitehead writes: "Apart from transmutation our feeble intellectual operations would fail to penetrate into the dominant characteristics of things. We can only understand by discarding" (PR 383). This is true not only of the operation whereby the macrocosmic emerges from the microcosmic, *but also of the operation whereby the macrocosmic is encountered as significant.* Horizontal transmutation is the operation productive of this latter significance. It is via vertical transmutation that the welter of actual occasions constitutive of a man are prehended as a unity, but it is in virtue of horizontal transmutation that significance is attached to the concept "man." Turning now to the aesthetic problem and utilizing horizontal transmutation to approach the notion of "ulteriority" will both clarify further the concept of horizontal transmutation and provide an introduction to the present theory of artistic creation.

Since it is to be used as an illustration, Frost's poem is included in full.[5]

STOPPING BY WOODS ON A SNOWY EVENING

Whose woods these are I think I know.
His house is in the village though;
He will not see me stopping here
To watch his woods fill up with snow.

5. *Complete Poems of Robert Frost* (New York, Holt; London, Cape; 1949), p. 275. By permission of the publishers.

My little horse must think it queer
To stop without a farmhouse near
Between the woods and frozen lake
The darkest evening of the year.

He gives his harness bells a shake
To ask if there is some mistake.
The only other sound's the sweep
Of easy wind and downy flake.

The woods are lovely, dark and deep,
But I have promises to keep,
And miles to go before I sleep,
And miles to go before I sleep.

I feel that Frost has captured exquisitely the experience one has occasionally of floating on the surface of one's own cosmic destiny, cut off from the world and seeming to drift aloof from all involvement for a brief spell, seeing oneself almost as a second person.

William James has written, "The pivot round which the religious life, as we have traced it, revolves, is the interest of the individual in his private personal destiny." [6] I would like to suggest that Frost has captured in his poem man's encounter with the religious dimension of experience.[7] This experience can come over one under various circumstances; in the blazing heat of a July cornfield miles from the farmhouse, or in the impersonal, eerie light of a subway car

6. *The Varieties of Religious Experience* (New York, New American Library of World Literature, 1958), p. 371.

7. By the religious dimension of experience I understand what John E. Smith and others mean when they speak of the religious dimension of a self in a world as being an inevitable drive which generates a question about and a concern for the ground and goal of human existence. The religious dimension of experience is to be distinguished from a positive religious faith; the former being a dimension of experience common to all men, the latter being a particular way of reacting to this fundamental dimension of experience. Frost would seem to be characterizing an awareness of the religious dimension of experience in this precise sense.

hurtling through a black tunnel. Frost undoubtedly has encountered this experience upon many occasions under very different circumstances. It is quite possible (though not necessary, nor even probable, given Frost's background) that he has never undergone this experience in a sleigh during a snowfall. Yet the genius of his poem is that he has embodied the religious dimension of experience in a striking setting that tends to reveal both the simplicity and the depth of the experience. The isolating and silencing effect of the snow, the contrast with the impatience of the horse, and the fleeting character of the mood that soon turns toward the promises that one must keep within this world's boundaries all heighten the suggestive character of the initial "Whose woods these are I think I know." Leading into the slow-moving, meditating line, "The woods are lovely, dark and deep," the poem altogether tends to thrust the reader toward the boundaries of his experience.

Horizontal transmutation is presupposed by the sense of ulteriority the poem conveys in the following way. The reading of the poem is not independent of past experiences. Certain past experiences have been akin to the immediate experience delivered by the poem. A reading of the poem allies itself with these other experiences. The aesthetic experience of the poem then fattens; it becomes "three-dimensional" in a sense; for the full proposition aesthetically re-created is a horizontally transmuted *intellectual* feeling as opposed to a transmuted *physical* feeling which results from vertical transmutation. This transmuted intellectual feeling adds a dimension of extra significance to experience; experience is significance, and extra significance is richness of experience. This transmuted intellectual feeling spreads over the entire family of related experiences, which are data for it, and transmutes this multiplicity of data into the one rich experience which is the experience of the ulteriority with which the poem is loaded.

To turn now to artistic creation, the role of horizontal transmutation in artistic creation can be exhibited by reversing the explanation of its role in aesthetic experience. Horizontal transmutation is the source of much creative inspiration. Creative artistic genius presupposes consistent horizontal transmutation of data in the reservoir of experience into richer, "three-dimensional" experience. In Chapter 3 I quoted Whitehead as follows: "Consciousness flickers; and even at its brightest, there is a small focal region of clear illumination, and a large penumbral region of experience which tells of intense experience in dim apprehension" (PR 408). The creative genius has the ability to exploit this dim, penumbral region. His experience is more intense than that of less gifted people in proportion to the breadth of his horizontal transmutation. Insofar as his conscious experiences incorporate horizontally transmuted elements, experience for him is shot through and through with significance. Whitehead writes:

> The human body is an instrument for the production of art in the life of the human soul. It concentrates upon those elements in human experiences selected for conscious perception [i.e. it heaps upon them via horizontal transmutations] intensities of subjective form derived from components dismissed into shadow. It thereby enhances the value of that appearance which is the subject matter for art. In this way the work of art is a message from the Unseen. It unlooses depths of feeling from behind the frontier where precision of consciousness fails. [AI 349]

This set of Whiteheadian categories provides a place in the make-up of man for the Platonic Muse; inspiration from the Unseen is here a precise, intelligible notion.[8] The

8. This analysis of "ulteriority" is supported by a passage from Edwyn Bevan's *Symbolism and Belief.* He writes: "it seems that the artist can sometimes secure that the object has that halo of association which con-

category of horizontal transmutation has been introduced as a category useful in Whitehead's regular account of knowing and then has been used to support a doctrine of artistic production based on his categories. The concept of creation introduced here is really broader than the notion of artistic creation. I maintain that horizontal transmutation is a factor in mathematical insight and scientific discovery, for instance, as well as a factor in artistic creation.[9] Horizontal transmutation underlies artistic creation, but it does not specify the characteristics of creative production that are specifically aesthetic. The remainder of this chapter will discover those characteristics of artistic creation that are uniquely artistic. This will require developing a theory closely related to the doctrines of Chapters 6 and 7.

11. ARTISTIC EXPRESSION

Chapter 3 clarified Whitehead's distinction between a physical purpose and a propositional feeling. In a physical

---

stitutes beauty *by making it remind us of something more or less definite other than itself.* If we do not attend to that other thing, or that other world of things, which the object suggests, *still the fact in itself that the object does suggest something other than itself may give us the sense that we are apprehending a world other than our ordinary everyday world . . .*" (Edwyn Bevan, *Symbolism and Belief*, Boston, Beacon Press, 1957, p. 277; my italics. See also pp. 143–46, 275–86.) Bevan, by noting that the art object reminds one of something more or less definite other than itself, is voicing an insight into the nature of "ulteriority" which parallels my own view.

9. It is therefore understandable that mathematicians have frequently likened their activities to artistic creation. Marston Morse writes: "The first essential bond between mathematics and the arts is found in the fact that discovery in mathematics is not a matter of logic. It is rather the result of mysterious powers which no one understands, and in which the unconscious recognition of beauty must play an important part. Out of an infinity of designs a mathematician chooses one pattern for beauty's sake, and pulls it down to earth, no one knows how" ("Mathematics and the Arts," *Yale Review*, 40 (1951), 607, quoted in Maritain, *Creative Intuition in Art and Poetry*, p. 307, n. 21). The present set of categories offers an explanation that preserves Morse's insight into the bond between mathematics and the arts.

purpose the predicate pried out of its immanence into transcendence at phase II of concrescence simply sinks back into integration with itself as immanent at phase III of concrescence and the initial conceptual contrast between potentiality and actuality vaporizes.[10] In a propositional feeling, however, the logical subject of its datum proposition has been reduced to the status of a mere logical subject and this reduction prevents the reintegration of the conceptual predicate with itself in a return to immanence, hence preparing the way for higher phases of concrescence and ultimately for the emergence of consciousness. The artist, above all, is concerned that the predicate which is the product of his horizontal transmutation should not sink back into immanence. His whole aim is to express that predicate forcefully, driving it firmly into consciousness. Hence he turns to propositions as vehicles for his artistic insights. A consideration of how the artist expresses his horizontal transmutation will serve to isolate artistic creation from creativity in general and also link this chapter with the two preceding ones.

A painter, for example, has an ordinary experience which horizontal transmutation enriches with added dimensions of significance. His problem is to capture those added dimensions of experience and express them. Were he simply to reproduce that ordinary experience, the dimensions added to his experience would evaporate. He has a unique transmuted predicate to express; this is his artistic problem. He must prevent this predicate from evaporating, from sinking back into one-dimensional immanence in the simpler experience which was its source.

I believe that the artistic problem is the problem of *expressing* that predicate, and by expressing that predicate I mean building it into a proposition. The product of horizontal transmutation is an "unqualified negation." It has

10. See above, p. 57.

been explained above [11] that an unqualified negation is a purely conceptual feeling, i.e. it is an unqualified negation in that it definitely extrudes any particular realization (PR 372). The added dimensions directly resulting from horizontal transmutation are unqualified negations. The predicates of horizontal transmutation are hence originally only dimly felt and the process of expression in art is the process of qualifying these negations by working them into propositions. Consciousness requires a contrast between potentiality and actuality; the full conscious awareness of the product of horizontal transmutations is possible only when these rich predicates have been fashioned into propositions whose logical subjects mediate the contrast with actuality. Expression in art, then, is the process of qualifying an unqualified negation. Expression is the discovery of a proposition which articulates the rich, yet irritatingly vague feelings arising from horizontal transmutation.

Frost's poem will be used to illustrate this doctrine. Let us suppose that Frost at some specific time experienced the sense of aloofness from the world, the withdrawal inwards from whence he looks out at himself and wonders about himself. This experience struck him with particular force; horizontal transmutation reinforced the feeling of the moment and he felt himself bursting with something significant, but wasn't yet sure just what it was or how to say it. Then slowly in stages, or maybe quickly all at once, he discovered the way to express that richness of feeling. The isolation of a snowstorm perhaps first suggested itself, then the further isolation of the contrast with a horse who lacks understanding, and the further overtones clinging to the idea of the shortest day of the year, etc., etc. This was the process of artistic expression, the process of discovering the subject which would revealingly embrace in an articulate proposition the significance generated by horizontal trans-

11. See above, p. 132.

mutation. The reader of Frost's poem is led down the reverse path toward articulate awareness of artistically revealed horizontal transmutations when he aesthetically recreates the proposition which is "Stopping by Woods."

III. CROCE

The ideas presented in the previous section are in some ways very similar to those of Benedetto Croce. In the present section I will clarify my own position by indicating some respects in which it is analogous to his theory and some respects in which it differs from his theory. I shall begin by presenting a criticism of Croce advanced by Ernst Cassirer; meeting Cassirer's difficulty will permit me to exhibit further certain aspects of my own theory. Cassirer writes:

> In many modern aesthetic theories—especially that of Croce and his disciples and followers—this material factor [i.e. the sensuous medium] is forgotten or minimized. Croce is interested only in the fact of expression, not in the mode. The mode he takes to be irrelevant both for the character and for the value of the work of art. The only thing which matters is the intuition of the artist, not the embodiment of this intuition in a particular material. The material has a technical but not an aesthetical importance. Croce's philosophy is a philosophy of the spirit emphasizing the purely spiritual character of the work of art. But in his theory the whole spiritual energy is contained and expended in the formation of the intuition alone. When this process is completed the artistic creation has been achieved. What follows is only an external reproduction which is necessary for the communication of the intuition but meaningless with respect to its essence. But for a great painter, a great musician, or a great

poet, the colors, the lines, rhythms, and words are not merely a part of his technical apparatus; they are necessary moments of the productive process itself.[12]

Like Croce, I am primarily interested in the fact of expression. But it is my contention that expression *does* involve, *in its essence*, "the colors, the lines, rhythms, and words." As was shown above, when Frost was engaged in the process of artistic expression which resulted in "Stopping by Woods," he worked with words and images in an effort to unlock the significance of his horizontal transmutations. The whole process of qualifying the originally unqualified negation which is the horizontal transmutation is a process of shaping an artistic medium to receive, and release, the significance of the transmutation. It certainly is an empirical fact that many composers compose at the piano and many painters search for ideas while dabbling in paints. The point is that they are searching for something, for the proposition that will support and clarify their yet imperfectly articulated horizontal transmutations. This playing around in the medium is not aimless, but is directed at releasing an insight; the insight is there and releasing it through the medium *is* artistic expression.

Crucial to this point is the fact that not all propositions are expressible in words. The propositions that interest the logician are those that are expressible in sentences like "It is raining" or "Il pleut." But this subclass of propositions does not exhaust the total class of propositions. There are propositions, i.e. lures for feeling, which express themselves *only in the various artistic media*. The anecdotes are legion in which a composer, for instance, curtly remarks to the obvious question that were he able to exhaust in words the expressive content of his composition he never would

12. *An Essay on Man* (New Haven, Yale University Press, 1944), pp. 141–42.

have bothered to write the music in the first place as it
would have been simpler just to rattle off the words and be
done with it. It is commonly acknowledged that a poem
cannot be exhausted by a prose paraphrase. How much less
so, then, a ballet, a painting, or a symphony. Each of these
expresses a proposition, a unique lure for feeling, which
involves, *in its essence*, "the colors, the lines, rhythms, and
words." It is obvious then, why artists compose in their
media; it is there that they find the propositions, the lures
for feeling, which receive and release their horizontal transmutations.

It is true, however, that, for example, many composers
do not compose at the piano. An acquaintance of mine who
arranges for a music company does all his work at a desk, utilizing no instrument at all, not even humming as far as I
can tell, yet he claims he can hear every bit of each orches-
tration clearly in his head and boasts of never having had
a manuscript returned. He does not play around in a
physical medium while composing, but it is apparent that
he does utilize what can be called the *conceived* medium.[13]
Likewise a painter may have "in his mind's eye" the proposition which is the art object, or he may have to experiment
on his canvas in order to discover the proposition that articulates his horizontal transmutation. It may be quite
true that a Michelangelo, for example, when he feels a
significance surrounding an experience and sets out to capture it in an artistic proposition, may not know initially
whether there is a painting or a statue on the way. But this
is my point against Cassirer; these inchoate feelings only
mature into artistic expression as a specific aesthetic medium, physical or conceived, is bent to receive and release
them. John Hospers echoes this point:

13. John Hospers makes this distinction in defending Croce's position
from an attack similar to that of Cassirer: "The Croce-Collingwood Theory
of Art," *Philosophy*, 31 (1956), 297.

In the most important sense, then, the Croce-Collingwood theory does not "institute a divorce" between intuition and medium at all: the intuition comes only *in* words or shapes or tones, and if it does not, then as far as art is concerned, the person is still in a state of "blooming buzzing confusion." The very thing, then, for which the theory is so often criticized—that of divorcing the intuition from the medium of expression —is exactly the reverse of the truth.[14]

And in my theory there is certainly no whisper of divorce, but only the holiest of marriages.

Going beyond Cassirer's specific objection, I maintain that the Crocean distinction between expression and externalization is a valid and useful distinction. Croce and Collingwood distinguish sharply, as Cassirer indicates, between the art process (or expression) on the one hand, and the craft process (or technique of external reproduction) on the other. This may be regarded as another way of phrasing my expression-performance distinction. In understanding this theory of artistic creation it is essential, if one would avoid confusion, to distinguish between artist and performer and to realize that it is the creativity of the artist that is being analyzed, and not that of the performer. The word "artist" is ambiguous. We frequently refer to Serkin and Cliburn as great artists. It would be less misleading to speak of them as "great keyboard artists." Properly speaking, Tchaikovsky is the artist and Cliburn the virtuoso; Beethoven the artist and Serkin the virtuoso.

My views have been criticized on this very point. It is objected that I fail to recognize the creative genius of

14. Ibid., p. 299. The Croce-Collingwood theory is, of course, developed in two classics of aesthetic analysis: Benedetto Croce's *Aesthetic*, New York, Noonday Press, 1958; and R. G. Collingwood's *The Principles of Art*, New York, Oxford University Press, Galaxy Book, 1958.

great actors, conductors, dancers, pianists, etc. I maintain
that I can, and do, recognize the genius of the virtuoso.
First, I shall insist that it is imperative to distinguish between the creative activity of the artist and that of the virtuoso. Surely any theory must be able to account for the
different senses in which Tchaikovsky and Cliburn create.
A more forceful example will make this point. Suppose for
the moment what may well in fact have been true, that
Hugo Wolf had no singing voice at all. On this supposition
it would have been impossible for him to have performed
his *lieder* himself. Hans Hotter, on the other hand, performs the Wolf *lieder* beautifully. Yet Hotter has, to my
knowledge, never composed vocal music; it can, in any
case, be assumed here that he has not. It is clear in this example that Wolf and Hotter are both creative, but in a
very different way, and theory must account for this difference. My distinction between expressing a proposition
and objectifying a proposition in a performance accounts
for this difference. If one wishes to refer to the activity of
Serkin, Cliburn, and Hotter as artistic creation, one can,
of course, do so, but in so doing there is the danger of
blurring the very real distinction that exists between the
creative activity of artist and virtuoso. In introducing the
machinery centering on the notion of horizontal transmutation I have been describing the creative activity of the
artist and not that of the virtuoso, and I will continue to
concentrate on artistic creation in what follows.

I shall, however, take a moment to adumbrate the manner in which the present theory does recognize the genius
of the virtuoso. It is true that the virtuoso is a technician,
a master craftsman, and the Croce-Collingwood theory is
certainly correct in pointing this out. But it is also true
that the virtuoso is more than a technician; technique is
not enough by itself. Superb technicians can be notoriously
inept performers, and any theory that implies that a great

performer is merely a technician does not deserve serious consideration. But the something more other than technique which the great performer has is a gift allied, not to the gift of the creative artist, but to that of the sensitive prehender of art. The great artist is the man who can unleash the significance only dimly felt in his horizontal transmutations by qualifying them to the logical subjects of particular aesthetic propositions. On the other hand, the man who responds sensitively to art (be he performer or not) travels the reverse path; art objects bring to a narrow focus his ordinary "two-dimensional" experience and transmute it horizontally into fattened, "three-dimensional" experience. The gift here is an openness to horizontal transmutation, whereas the gift of the artist is the ability to exploit the dim, penumbral region of horizontal transmutations by fixing them, by qualifying them to specific propositions. The great performer is the one whose sensitivity to horizontal transmutation guides his objectifications unerringly to the crest of their respective hillocks, releasing the full transmutational power of the propositions they express.

This view is supported by an item from my own experience. A college classmate was a gifted technician at the piano; produce any score and he had the notes brilliantly under control. He had played private recitals for Harold Bauer, José Iturbi, and other eminent masters and to a man their advice was the same—go get a liberal arts college education, then come back to the concert stage. In the light of the present theory this advice makes sense. A liberal arts education provides insight into the trials and aspirations of men; it provides the sort of experience required by art. Unless these experiences are brought to art, art cannot generate horizontal transmutations. These experiences are required, for example, in order to appreciate Shakespeare's dramas, and this explains why we can go back to Shake-

speare year after year and discover more and more in his
art each time we read him; we bring to him a progressively
richer basis for horizontal transmutations. These experiences are required for all and any aesthetic experience, but
above all are they required for the man who would objectify
propositions in a way so as to release transmutations in his
audience. It should be noted how far away this view is
from Clive Bell's dictum, cited above, that "to appreciate
a work of art we need bring with us nothing from life."
These considerations are relevant to the discussion of the
function of art in Chapter 10, but for the moment it suffices to have given an account of the genius of the virtuoso which does the virtuoso justice and yet at the same
time distinguishes his creative activity from that of the
artist.

It is worth remarking that many individuals have concentrated in their person both the gift of the artist and the
gift of the virtuoso. I need only mention Frederic Chopin,
Martha Graham, Leonard Bernstein, Peter Ustinov, Gene
Kelly, José Iturbi, and Robert Frost. The fact that in the
performer arts many individuals are gifted as both artists
and virtuosos leads to the further point that in the nonperformer arts, because there exists in these arts no system
of notation whereby the painter or sculptor can formalize
his intuitions as rules for performances,[15] the artist must
necessarily be virtuoso as well. Those painters and sculptors
who articulate horizontal transmutations in the conceived
medium must have the technique of objectifying them if
they would share their aesthetic insights, while for those,
particularly abstractionists, who create in the physical medium, skill in controlling the medium is essential to the

15. The clavilux, a keyboard instrument which controls the play of
colored lights on a screen, is an interesting instrument because it has generated a painting-like art form which is still a performer art where a system
of notation exists enabling the "painter" to formalize his intuitions as rules
for performing which can be executed by a virtuoso.

creative process itself. Whereas a Hugo Wolf could succeed in the performer arts while lacking any technique
for objectification, it is necessary for the painter or sculptor to possess such technique in addition to the distinctively
artistic gift.

The importance of seizing on expression and emphasizing it is that it isolates the unique element in artistic creation from periphery elements in the art process. Hospers
has made this point clearly.

As we have observed, common usage of language
associates the term "expression" with the process of
externalization rather than with the process of intuition. When Croce repudiates this, refusing to call the
first process "expression" and applying the term only
to the second process, what (one might ask) is this
but sheer terminological perversity?

It is no doubt true that this reversal of terms has
caused considerable confusion in the minds of introductory students in aesthetics. It is also probably true
that what Croce gives us is a persuasive definition of
"expression": he uses the emotively-tinged term to refer to the activity to which he attaches the most importance. But there are reasons for considering it more
important: for if we may assume (what the majority
of critics would probably believe without question)
that the distinctive activity of the artist is that of expression, then what Croce is insisting on is that this
distinctive activity has to do with the genesis or coming-into-being of the artist's intuitions and not of his
externalizations. And if this is so, those who talk of
the artist's "ability to express" as if it were simply
"skill in handling a medium" (e.g. the slick journalist,
the advertising artist) are simply in error, and Croce
is pointing out this error to us.[16]

16. Hospers, pp. 294–95.

Like Croce, I want to insist through my doctrine that the distinctive activity of the artist has to do with the coming-into-being of his intuitions, a process I have described in my own terms in section II of this chapter.

I turn now to another, but related, aspect of the Croce-Collingwood theory, the doctrine that there are no unexpressed artistic intuitions. Hospers writes:

> Wordsworth said that there are many poets in the world who have "the vision and faculty divine, yet wanting the accomplishment of verse"; if this means that they have a "vision" but "the words just won't come to them," Croce and Collingwood would unhesitatingly say that they do not have *poetic* intuitions at all. . . .
>
> Another way of putting this is to say that according to the theory there are no "mute inglorious Miltons," poets who cannot find the words to express what they feel. Many persons, perhaps the majority of mankind, have feelings of great intensity and depth, and the artist is not distinguished from other men by his capacity to have them, but rather by his power of expressing them (even if only to himself) *in a medium.* Mozart probably had no more intense emotions of exultation, bereavement, or melancholy than his siblings and cousins, but he was a composer and they were not because he could express his emotions in the musical medium and they could not. If they were mute, *ipso facto* they were not Miltons.[17]

My own interpretation of this point is as follows. The phenomenon of horizontal transmutation is widespread; as Hospers notes, "perhaps the majority of mankind" have feelings three-dimensionally significant as a result of horizontal transmutation. But these feelings are normally vague

17. Ibid., pp. 297–98.

and inarticulate. The artist is the individual who, in Croce's terminology, expresses these feelings *"in a medium,"* i.e. discovers a proposition with its logical subject grounded in the artistic medium which serves to support and hence *articulate* the predicate of horizontal transmutation. The person who prehends an objectified proposition aesthetically prehends that performance with the subjective aim of re-creating in the immediacy of his own experience the proposition objectified in the performance. Subjectively re-creating the proposition which is the art object *articulates for the contemplator* the extra dimensions of feeling he himself may well possess as a result of horizontal transmutation but which have most likely been vague and inarticulate feelings from a dim, penumbral region.

A final aspect of the Crocean theory that my view approximates is an aspect where I think my account proves superior to that of Croce. I refer now to the subject matter of Chapter 6, the ontological status of the art object. Like Croce, I have a theory in which the account of artistic creation, of expression, leads to the position that the work of art is not the physical artifact, as is popularly supposed. Croce holds that the work of art is something that exists in the mind of the artist; that the artifact is only a means toward the end of permitting those who experience it to reproduce it in their own minds. On this latter point I agree with Croce. But Croce's view has certain difficulties. As Hospers notes, "If one conceives the work of art as something in the artist's mind, one must accept the consequence that it no longer exists when the artist dies or is asleep or not thinking about it . . ." [18] But on the present theory it is clear that if the artist dies, or sleeps or thinks of other things, the propositional status of the art object is not affected one whit. In section II of Chapter 6 I quoted Whitehead as follows: "the physical feeling, which is always one

18. Ibid., p. 299.

component in the history of an integral propositional feeling has no unique relation to the proposition in question,
*nor has the subject of that feeling, which is also a subject
prehending the proposition"* (PR 396, my italics). If the
artist dies or sleeps, the proposition which is the art object
still enjoys its categoreal type of existence; it is still a lure
for feeling.

IV. GOD AND ARTISTIC CREATION

The foregoing sections have provided a precise interpretation for certain of the phrases in Forster's metaphor,
phrases such as "the underworld," "obscure recesses of our
being," and "dips a bucket down." It remains to show in
what sense God is a "common quality" and in what sense
the creative artist approaches "the gates of the Divine."

It was noted in Chapter 3 that only God can conjure up
conceptual feelings that do not depend upon prior physical
feelings: "Unfettered conceptual valuation, 'infinite' in
Spinoza's sense of that term, is only possible once in the
universe; since that creative act is objectively immortal as
an inescapable condition characterizing creative action"
(PR 378). The artist does not create *ex nihilo*, or out of
whole cloth; his vision is not "unfettered," or "infinite" as
is that of God. Yet his vision is productive of "the light
that never was, on sea or land." [19] The artist is not God,
and his creative activity presupposes God in the same
sense that all advance into novelty presupposes God. From
the standpoint of "sea or land," from the point of view of
actuality, the artist is a discoverer. Here I must place my
own theory in opposition to that of Croce, who maintains
that artistic creation implies absolute novelty and a bring-
ing into being *ex nihilo*. The artist does not create a proposition *ex nihilo*, he discovers a proposition.[20] The proposi-

19. See above, p. 50.
20. See the passage from Leclerc quoted above, p. 26.

tion, through its logical subject, is related to a context; it
refers to preexistents in terms of which it can be understood. Without this contextual relationship creation would
be unintelligible; this is, in fact, the argument used by
Milton Nahm in rejecting Croce's *ex nihilo* theory of artistic creation.[21] Nahm's objection to Croce is built squarely
into the present theory in the following way: reversions
play a crucial role in artistic creation (a role to be specified
immediately) and it is characteristic of a reversion that it
is *partially identical with*, as well as partially diverse from,
the datum prehended at phase I of concrescence which
"triggers" that reversion.[22]

It will be recalled from Chapter 3 that a reversion is a
conceptual feeling arising in phase II of concrescence
which is partially identical with and partially diverse from
the eternal objects constitutive of the datum prehended in
phase I. Hume's missing shade of blue is hence a conceptual reversion. But the point was made in Chapter 3 [23]
that in the final analysis Hume's dictum that "all our
ideas, or weak perceptions, are derived from our impressions or strong perceptions" [24] remains without exception.
In the last analysis a conceptual reversion depends upon
the hybrid physical feeling of God that is part of phase I
of every concrescence. Whitehead writes:

> Thus, a more fundamental account must ascribe the
> reverted conceptual feeling in a temporal subject to

21. *The Artist as Creator* (Baltimore, Johns Hopkins University Press,
1956), chaps. 7, 8, 12.

22. See the subsection, "Conceptual Reversion," above, pp. 51–53, and
PR 380–82. At PR 381 Whitehead writes: "reversion is always limited by
the necessary inclusion of elements identical with elements in feelings of
the antecedent phase."

23. Above, p. 52.

24. David Hume, *An Abstract of a Treatise of Human Nature*, published as a supplement to *An Inquiry Concerning Human Understanding*
(New York, Liberal Arts Press, 1955), p. 185.

its conceptual feeling derived, according to Category IV, from the hybrid physical feeling of the relevancies conceptually ordered in God's experience. In this way, by the recognition of God's characterization of the creative act, a more complete rational explanation is attained. The category of reversion is then abolished; and Hume's principle of the derivation of conceptual experience from physical experience remains without any exception. [PR 382]

In the preceding paragraph I have related conceptual reversions to God. I shall now relate conceptual reversions to the theory of artistic creation presented in sections ɪ and ɪɪ above. It will then be a simple matter to indicate God's relationship to the process of artistic creation.

My theory is that the horizontal transmutations which bear the extra significance expressed by the artist in the process of artistic creation are composed in part of conceptual reversions. The extra dimensions of significance which cloak certain experiences and call for artistic release are built up by a transmutation that has as its data not only past related experiences but also reversions based on those experiences. God's relationship to artistic creation is therefore clear; God is the source of novel dimensions incorporated into the horizontal transmutations which it is the task of the creative genius to express artistically. In sections ɪ and ɪɪ of this chapter I concentrated on horizontal transmutation as "fattening" already given experience. It is certainly true that already given experiences are important in horizontal transmutation, and here lies the importance for aesthetic experience of what we bring from the world to art. But as it there stood the doctrine of artistic creation is incomplete, for the addition of reverted feelings is absolutely essential. It is in this sense that art is larger than life. The earlier account provided the machinery for horizontal transmutation; the doctrine of reversions adds the content which completes the theory.

The artist is creative of true novelty in the sense that the horizontal transmutations he seeks to express embody "the light that never was, on sea or land." Yet it is correct metaphysically to characterize the artist as a discoverer rather than creator for the sake of distinguishing his activity from that of God's infinite conceptual visualization. As discoverer he still brings into actual being that which is not yet actual and that which has not yet been prehended as relevant by any temporal being. Forster, it will be recalled, looked back "with longing to the earlier modes of criticism where a poem was not an expression but a discovery, and was sometimes supposed to have been shown to the poet by God." Forster's longing to characterize artistic creation as a discovery is a valid insight as a way of distinguishing the artist from God, and certainly I have specified here a precise sense in which a poem is "shown" to the poet by God. On the other hand, I have at the same time retained a doctrine of creative expression which does justice to the artist's empirical feeling of creative productivity. Writing about Bergson's theory, Hulme remarks:

> The process of artistic creation would be better described as a process of discovery and disentanglement. To use the metaphor which one is by now so familiar with—the stream of the inner life, and the definite crystallised shapes on the surface—the big artist, the creative artist, the innovator, leaves the level where things are crystallised out into these definite shapes, and, diving down into the inner flux, comes back with a new shape which he endeavors to fix. He cannot be said to have created it, but to have discovered it, because when he has definitely expressed it we recognise it as true.[25]

25. *Speculations*, p. 149.

The metaphysical justification for my use of the notion of discovery is somewhat different from Hulme's, but his phraseology as precedent makes my terminology that much less strange. The concept of artistic creation as discovery, in the precise sense here given to that term, is in fact a corollary of the doctrine of Chapter 6 that the art object is a proposition; propositions are lures for feeling and the artist discovers a proposition which has been luring him when he molds his artistic medium in such a way as to unite the horizontally transmuted predicate, the significance of which has been luring him into creative activity, with the logical subject that supports and releases that significance.

These paragraphs have specified the sense in which the creative artist approaches "the gates of the Divine." The whole chapter has been designed to show that divine inspiration is not something appealed to *ad hoc* in this system; rather, in the spirit of Maritain's exhortation, I have shown that it is the underlying metaphysical requirement linking the creative surge of actuality in all its gradations, from God to "the most trivial puff of existence in far-off empty space" (PR 28), with the infinite possibilities visualized in God's primordial conceptual valuation. Artistic creation is simply a more concentrated, sophisticated version of an activity common to all actual occasions; "a place is prepared in the highest parts of the soul" for a rational, intelligible account of artistic creation.

9. Truth in Art

WHITEHEAD's view that the logician's account of propositions expresses only a restricted aspect of their role in the universe has already been cited.[1] In a striking passage he makes this point by a direct reference to the arts.

> It is evident, however, that the primary function of theories is as a lure for feeling, thereby providing immediacy of enjoyment and purpose. Unfortunately theories, under their name of 'propositions,' have been handed over to logicians, who have countenanced the doctrine that their one function is to be judged as to their truth or falsehood. . . . The existence of imaginative literature should have warned logicians that their narrow doctrine is absurd. It is difficult to believe that all logicians as they read Hamlet's speech, "To be, or not to be: . . ." commence by judging whether the initial proposition be true or false, and keep up the task of judgment throughout the whole thirty-five lines. Surely, at some point in the reading, judgment is eclipsed by aesthetic delight. The speech, for the theatre audience, is purely theoretical, a mere lure for feeling.
>
> Again, consider strong religious emotion—consider a Christian meditating on the sayings in the Gospels. He is not judging 'true or false'; he is eliciting their

1. See above, p. 106.

value as elements in feeling. In fact, he may ground
his judgment of truth upon his realization of value.
But such a procedure is impossible, if the primary
function of propositions is to be elements in judgments. [PR 281]

It is the contention of the present theory that Whitehead
is making a valid protest and that works of art constitute
a class of propositions significant in virtue of exhibiting the
primary propositional characteristic of being lures for feeling.

But this view raises an important question. Even if works
of art are propositions functioning in their primary role as
lures for feeling, what is the relation, qua proposition, of a
work of art to truth and falsehood? Certainly it is not uncommon to link the notions of art and truth. It is not at
all unusual to hear or read that the truths of art are eternal;
one has but to recall Keats and the Grecian Urn. How,
then, are the propositions which are art objects related, if
at all, to the notion of truth?

Answering this question requires first of all an account
of truth. Whitehead remarks that "in the realm of truth
there are many mansions" (AI 314). Not all these senses
of truth can be specified here. The chapter titled "Truth"
in *Adventures of Ideas* (pp. 309–23) spells out in detail
the various types of truth-relation that can hold between
appearance and reality. I shall present only the type required by my theory of the role played by truth in art.

The distinction between appearance and reality is crucial. "Truth is a qualification which applies to Appearance
alone. Reality is just itself, and it is nonsense to ask whether
it be true or false. Truth is the conformation of Appearance to Reality" (AI 309). Where, in Whitehead's system, is reality located and where is appearance located?
Chapter 2 clearly made the point that the really real for

Whitehead is the actual occasion. Nexūs, groupings of occasions, are abstractions, and to attribute full reality to them is to commit the Fallacy of Misplaced Concreteness.[2] Chapter 3, in describing concrescence, indicated the mechanism by which complex occasions, starting with prehensions of microcosmic actual occasions, move to intellectual feelings of macrocosmic entities—trees, houses, stones, etc. The microcosmic actual occasions prehended at the first phase of concrescence constitute reality; the macrocosmic entities prehended at the fourth phase constitute appearance. "The unconscious entertainment of propositions is a stage in the transition from the Reality of the initial phase of experience to the Appearance of the final phase" (AI 313).

Now that appearance and reality have been specified, the nature of truth in its most important sense can be elucidated. "In human experience, clear and distinct Appearance is primarily sense-perception" (AI 321). Sensa are eternal objects of the subjective species, i.e. they qualify subjective form, they are the way concrescing occasions feel their data, they are "qualifications of affective tone" (AI 314). Sensa are "primarily inherited as such qualifications and then by 'transmutation' are objectively perceived as qualifications of regions" (AI 315); i.e. though eternal objects of the subjective species, they acquire a secondary role as functioning objectively.[3] The truth relationship follows:

> the sensum as a factor in the datum of a prehension imposes itself as a qualification of the affective tone which is the subjective form of that prehension. Thus a pattern of affective tone is conformally produced by a pattern of sensa as datum. Now when a region ap-

2. See above, p. 59.
3. See above, p. 28.

pears as red in sense-perception, the question arises
whether red is qualifying in any dominant manner the
affective tones of the actualities which in fact make up
the region.

If so, there is in this sense a truth-relation between
the reality of the region and its appearance for the
contemporary percipient. [AI 315]

This is the central meaning of truth, what Whitehead
calls "blunt truth" (AI 321). But this is not the exact sense
in which truth is relevant for art. This is the straightfor-
ward, literal sense of truth, and is not the precise sense
we are using when we refer to truth in art. In this "blunt"
sense of truth, falsehoods are of great aesthetic importance
—grass in paintings need not be green; people in novels
need not act as our neighbors do. A man couldn't wake up
one morning as a cockroach, but Kafka's story is a work
of art.[4] The sense of truth which *is* relevant to art must
now be specified.

Sense perception results in "clear and distinct Appearance"; blunt truth is the truth relevant to this clear and
distinct appearance. But the truths of art are not blunt
truths, they are dim, massive truths.

> The deliverances of clear and distinct consciousness
> require criticism by reference to elements in experi-
> ence which are neither clear nor distinct. On the con-
> trary, they are dim, massive, and important. These
> dim elements provide for art that final background of
> tone apart from which its effects fade. The type of
> Truth which human art seeks lies in the eliciting of

4. This example from Kafka was used by Abraham Kaplan to make
the same point in the second of his three Matchette Lectures at Wesleyan
University in April 1960. These stimulating lectures have not, to my
knowledge, been published, but Professor Kaplan's remarks parallel my
own views in a significant manner on this question of truth in art.

this background to haunt the object presented for clear consciousness. [AI 348]

Let me explain this point in my own words. Reality is a surging mass of microcosmic feelings, of microcosmic emotional colors. The transmutation which leads away from the microcosmic to the macrocosmic is an elimination and a distortion; abstraction leaves something out, but we must abstract. The proposition which is a given work of art has transmuted *macro*cosmic entities as logical subjects and transmuted *macro*cosmic, i.e. clear and recognizable, feelings and emotions in its predicative patterns. These patterns can be either true or false in the blunt, clear sense of truth. But they are aesthetically true only if they are compatible with, conformable to, eductive of the massive but dim emotional patterns at the *micro*cosmic level which surge through the relevant realities. A predicate that is bluntly, clearly false can be aesthetically true in the highest degree; the Kafka story is a good example, or Shakespeare's *The Tempest*, or Picasso's "Man with an All-Day Sucker."

This concept of aesthetic truth has important consequences for the theory of beauty presented in Chapter 8. There a one-dimensional theory of beauty was presented, a theory of beauty as exemplified in appearance alone. The way is now open for a two-dimensional theory of beauty, a theory of aesthetically truthful beauty.

> Beauty, so far as concerns its exemplification in Appearance alone, does not necessarily involve the attainment of truth. Appearance is beautiful when the qualitative objects which compose it are interwoven in patterned contrasts, so that the prehensions of the whole of its parts produces the fullest harmony of mutual support. . . .
> It is evident that when appearance has obtained

truth in addition to beauty, harmony in a wider sense
has been produced. For in this sense, it also involves
the relation of appearance to reality. Thus, when the
adaptation of appearance to reality has obtained truthful Beauty, there is a perfection of art. [AI 344–45]

Beauty is the mutual adaptation of the several factors in
an occasion of experience; it is the harmony of synthesis in
the subjective form of experience. Theories of Art for Art's
Sake would seem to operate simply at the level of appearance, to be concerned with the various elements in appearance. The present theory goes beyond this view. Truthful beauty is the harmony resulting from a conformation,
a syncretism, between appearance and reality, between the
clear, articulate patterns that characterize conscious experience and the dim, massive patterns throbbing through
the microcosmic realm. Art is not a realm apart, it is a realm
indissolubly linked to the world, to reality.

Beauty, in this deep-flowing sense of truthful beauty,
allows for an account of the aesthetic significance of the
ugly. The ugly can be aesthetically significant in the same
sense that the "bluntly" false can be aesthetically significant. The ugliness involved is ugliness contained solely in
the realm of appearance. Bluntly false predicates can be
aesthetically true in the highest degree because eductive of
the massive but dim emotional patterns at the microcosmic
level. Likewise, "bluntly" ugly predicates can be beautiful
in the deep-flowing sense because eductive of a syncretism
between appearance and reality productive of higher harmonies that transcend the discords at the level of appearance. One thinks of *Richard III* and Peter Breughel's "The
Blind Leading the Blind."

A final point needs to be made about this theory, a crucial point paralleling the dimension of reversions added

to the theory of artistic creation in section IV of Chapter 8. The point is that the theory is not a backward-looking, static theory, but incorporates a dynamic thrust toward novelty. Whitehead makes this point powerfully:

> The type of Truth required for the final stretch of Beauty is a discovery and not a recapitulation. The Truth that for such extremity of Beauty is wanted is that truth-relation whereby Appearance summons up new resources of feeling from the depths of Reality. It is a Truth of feeling, and not a Truth of verbalization. The relata in Reality must lie below the stale presuppositions of verbal thought. The Truth of supreme Beauty lies beyond the dictionary meanings of words. [AI 343]

The new resources summoned up appear in the form of reversions, as described in the last chapter.

This passage ties together and undergirds several of the points made in previous chapters. It supports the doctrine that horizontal transmutations involving reversions are at the heart of artistic creation, because it reveals that these horizontal reversions are "loaded with ulteriority" in that their "thickness" consists in part of overtones of massive but dim feelings which flow closer to consciousness when appearances are "fattened" by horizontal transmutation. In emphasizing truths of feeling as opposed to truths of verbalization it emphasizes that the propositions which are art objects are propositions exhibiting their primary characteristic of being lures for feeling. In specifying a precise sense in which new resources of feeling are summoned from the depths of reality, it goes a long way toward providing an answer to Forster's query as to "What there is down there."

In the course of this discussion of the role of truth in

art a rebuttal of Art for Art's Sake aesthetics emerged from the concepts employed. In the next chapter I shall turn to the question of the function of art directly and argue for an Art for Life's Sake theory which can also incorporate some of the major points of the Art for Art's Sake view.

10. The Function of Art

THE theory emerging from Whitehead's categories is not basically a theory of Art for Art's Sake. It is, rather, a theory of Art for Life's Sake such as that characterized by Iredell Jenkins in the following phrases: "it is my thesis that aesthetic activity is a natural and spontaneous phase of man's ordinary response to the environment; that it is a necessary partner in the process of adjustment; that art exists for life's sake, and that life could not exist without art." [1] I shall indicate how the Whiteheadian categories lead to the sort of theory advocated by Jenkins.

I first want to point out that Whitehead himself has offered some observations concerning the function of art. They seem to me to be neither profound nor suggestive. His line of thought is contained in the following passages:

> But the secret of art lies in its freedom. The emotion and some elements of the experience itself are lived again divorced from their necessity. The strain is over, but the joy of intense feeling remains. Originally the intensity arose from some dire necessity; but in art it has outlived the compulsion which was its origin. . . .
>
> The arts of civilization now spring from many origins, physical and purely imaginative. But they are all

1. *Art and the Human Enterprise* (Cambridge, Harvard University Press, 1958), p. 4.

sublimations, and sublimations of sublimations, of the simple craving to enjoy freely the vividness of life which first arises in moments of necessity. With a slight shift of the focus of our attention, Art can be described as a psychopathic reaction of the race to the stresses of its existence. [AI 350]

This is a fairly definite theory, borrowing heavily from Aristotle and Freud. My dissatisfaction with it stems from its backward-looking character. Whitehead has a system in which the emphasis is on the dynamic surge into ever fresh novelty, and one would expect from such a system a more dynamic account of the function of art.

There is, however, in another suggestion made by Whitehead, an indication of a much more satisfying account:

The work of Art is a fragment of nature with the mark on it of a finite creative effort, so that it stands alone, an individual thing detailed from the vague infinity of its background. Thus Art heightens the sense of humanity. It gives an elation of feeling which is supernatural. A sunset is glorious, but it dwarfs humanity and belongs to the general flow of nature. A million sunsets will not spur on men towards civilization. It requires Art to evoke into consciousness the finite perfections which lie ready for human achievement. [AI 348]

If this suggestion about spurring men on to greater finite perfections could be worked out into a theory of the function of art, it would provide an account more in keeping with the Whiteheadian system. This I will try to do in what follows. But I also want to point out that the categories developed in Chapter 7 above permit me to specify a limited though important sense in which the present theory does justice to some of the insights that are incorporated into the Art for Art's Sake position. I will first indicate how the arguments advanced in *The Function of Reason* provide a foundation for an Art for Life's Sake theory. Then I will advance some considerations which are quite compatible with this theory but which embody some of the major insights of the Art for Art's Sake position.

1. ART FOR LIFE'S SAKE

In *The Function of Reason* Whitehead takes issue with an *unreflective* interpretation of the theory of evolution. He wants to know why organic species would ever have developed in the first place if the theory were true as baldly stated; inorganic things persist for long periods compared even with trees. "It may be possible to explain 'the origin of species' by the doctrine of the struggle for existence among such organisms. But certainly this struggle throws no light whatever upon the emergence of such a general type of complex organism, with faint survival power" (FR 5). Whitehead is fully prepared to recognize that the doctrine has "its measure of truth"; in fact, he characterizes it as "one of the great generalizations of science" (FR 6). But he maintains that in trying to stretch it to explain everything, enthusiasts have made it explain nothing. "Why has the trend of evolution been upwards? The fact that organic species have been produced from inorganic distributions of matter, and the fact that in the lapse of time organic species of higher and higher types have evolved are not in the least explained by any doctrine of adaptation to the environment, or of struggle" (FR 7). Whitehead emphasizes, rather, that those species which have "actively engaged in modifying their environment" have spearheaded the upward trend. He recognizes that "all these operations [of modifying the environment] are meant by the common doctrine of adaptation to the environment. But they are very inadequately expressed by that

statement; and the real facts easily drop out of sight under cover of that statement" (FR 8). Whitehead's aim is
to emphasize these "real facts," for it is in the course of
explaining these "real facts" that his doctrine of the function of Reason emerges.

> I now state the thesis that the explanation of this
> active attack on the environment is a three-fold urge:
> (i) to live, (ii) to live well, (iii) to live better. In fact
> the art of life is *first* to be alive, *secondly* to be alive
> in a satisfactory way, and *thirdly* to acquire an in-
> crease in satisfaction. It is at this point of our argu-
> ment that we have to recur to the function of Reason,
> namely the promotion of the art of life. The primary
> function of Reason is the direction of the attack on
> the environment.
> This conclusion amounts to the thesis that Reason
> is a factor in experience which directs and criticizes the
> urge towards the attainment of an end realized in
> imagination but not in fact. [FR 8]

Reason as thus conceived is the great countertendency
operative in the course of events, the tendency in the universe counter to the slow decay of physical nature.

> Apart from anarchic appetition, nature is doomed to
> slow descent towards nothingness. Mere repetitive ex-
> perience gradually eliminates element after element
> and fades towards vacuity. . . . Mental experience is
> the organ of novelty, the urge beyond. It seeks to vivify
> the massive physical fact, which is repetitive, with the
> novelties which beckon. Thus mental experience con-
> tains in itself a factor of anarchy. . . . [However]
> mere anarchic appetition [only] accomplishes quickly
> the same end, reached slowly by repetition. . . . [To

prevent this,] mentality now becomes self-regulative. It canalizes its own operations by its own judgments. It introduces a higher appetition which discriminates among its own anarchic productions. . . . Reason civilizes the brute force of anarchic appetition. . . . Reason is the special embodiment in us of the disciplined counter-agency which saves the world. [FR 33–34]

I can now specify the way in which the Whiteheadian categories lead to a theory of Art for Life's Sake. The horizontal transmutations described in Chapter 8, which are expressed in the propositions which are art objects, have extra dimensions of significance. The transmutation involved and the presence of reversions guarantee that these transmuted intellectual feelings embrace great depth of contrast. Depth of contrast is the gauge of depth of satisfaction; hence anything leading to a depth of contrast leads to a depth of satisfaction. Therefore, since the art of life is the art of acquiring an increase in satisfaction, commerce with art constitutes the apex of the art of life. There are some men who merely live, others who enjoy some satisfactions, and some few who are able to attain the very highest of human satisfactions. Art plays a prominent role in the lives of these latter, generating the depth of satisfaction they enjoy. This is the first important sense in which the Whiteheadian categories embrace an Art for Life's Sake view of the function of art.

But Whitehead's doctrine of Reason has indicated another aspect of this doctrine of Art for Life's Sake. Reason directs "the attack on the environment" by criticizing and directing "the urge towards the attainment of an end realized in imagination but not in fact." Art is the mode of entrance *par excellence* into the imagination of ends worthy of attainment. Not of ends such as bigger automobiles or automatic washing machines, but of ends such as love and respect of neighbor for neighbor, maturity, self-discipline, etc. Other men constitute the single most important aspect of the human environment, and art is perhaps the most important means by which men have succeeded to the extent that they have in modifying this aspect of their environment.[2] *The Bible, The Divine Comedy, Paradise Lost* —these are works of art which express ends realized in the imagination of their authors but not in fact which have served as lures over the centuries for mankind in its struggle against the human environment. Reason through art "introduces a higher appetition" which "civilizes" the brutish and anarchic appetitions of men. "A million sunsets will not spur on men towards civilization," but art does.

These considerations suffice to indicate the sense in which the Whiteheadian categories are capable of supporting a theory of Art for Life's Sake. The sense in which these categories incorporate some of the important insights of the Art for Art's Sake theory is much less obvious. Nevertheless, I maintain that the Art for Art's Sake view *does* contain important insights into the function of art. I shall now indicate how my theory of aesthetic experience permits me to include these insights in the present theory in a manner compatible with the material presented so far in this chapter.

2. Stephen Pepper, in analyzing a picture that arouses feelings of sadness, pity, and indignation, notes: "Furthermore, these different emotions at once intrude upon and restrain one another, so that we feel the event deeply and yet do not take the picture as a piece of propaganda or begin to think about practical action. On the contrary, the social conflict suggested becomes itself a factor of enhancement fusing with the contrasts of color and line and mass. And at the same time (art is so full of paradoxes) the full realization of this event because of its restraint and because of its very intrinsic beauty *acts in the long run as more powerful propaganda than propaganda*" (*Aesthetic Quality*, pp. 102–3; my italics).

11. Art for Art's Sake

Artists, critics, and aestheticians all frequently employ the phrase, "the realm of art," or similar phrases. E. M. Forster, for example, in the long quotation that introduces Part II of this essay, speaks of the "world created by words." It is not a simple matter to assign precise meaning to these phrases, but they and others like them are widely used and would seem to point toward an important aspect of aesthetic experience. The theory presented in these chapters provides a set of categories capable of interpreting these metaphors and offering a precise explication of the aesthetic truth lying behind them.

It is quite common in ordinary speech for someone to say, for example: "If you enter the 'realm' of business, if you throw yourself into the financial 'world,' you may lose contact with the finer things in life." Such a warning obviously intends to inform a young man that the pursuit of wealth and influence is so intense that it can easily become a dominating *aim* that crowds every other consideration out of life. Sports offer another example. Boxing as a profession can absorb all a man's energy, as can professional tennis or even amateur golf.

I wish to suggest that the linking of the notion of a "realm" on the one hand and an "aim" on the other, which occurs in the above paragraph is perfectly natural and that going one step further and analyzing the notion of an "aim" in terms of Whitehead's category "subjective aim" can produce some important conclusions concerning the precise meaning that the notion "realm of art" is capable of acquiring.

Human existence usually occupies several "realms" simultaneously; i.e. people normally pursue various overlapping aims. Usually there is a dominant aim, directed at one's vocation, which satisfies the aim of providing food,

clothing, and shelter. Then there are the realms of family
"togetherness," this sport, that hobby, community service,
etc., which in a fortunately balanced and happily endowed
existence are organized about a dominant aim which com-
bines self-development with breadwinning. People are resident in the realms in which they participate in virtue of
their aims—some goal, some purpose to be achieved; this
is what makes the everyday notion of the realm of this or
that significant.

The central point I want to make is that the art object
breaks into and suspends these normal aims of everyday
living. Aesthetic experience is aesthetic just because these
various aims of practical living are suspended. In grasping
the subjective aim of one who experiences it aesthetically,
the art object insists that it be experienced as an end in
itself, i.e. it temporarily short-circuits, if you will, the long-
range, overarching subjective aims that shape life patterns
and dominate ordinary living. Herbert Spencer has written
in this same vein.

> Throughout the whole range of sensations, percep-
> tions, and emotions which we do not class as aesthetic,
> the states of consciousness serve simply as aids and
> stimuli to guidance and action. They are transitory,
> or if they persist in consciousness some time, they do
> not monopolize the attention: that which monop-
> olizes the attention is something ulterior, to the ef-
> fecting of which they are instrumental. But in the
> states of mind we class as aesthetic, the opposite atti-
> tude is maintained towards the sensations, percep-
> tions, and emotions. *These are no longer links in the
> chain of states which prompt and guide conduct.*[3]

The everyday aims are temporarily ignored as one strives
in the activity of aesthetic contemplation to re-create in

3. *Principles of Psychology* (New York, Appleton, 1871), 2, 646–47.
My italics.

subjective immediacy the proposition objectified in the prehended performance. I submit that it is this suspension of ordinary aims, recognized by Spencer, and the presence of re-creative aim at the art object which together grant access to the "realm of art" and are presupposed by Forster's discussion of the "world created by words." It is interesting to note that Forster remarks that whether or not words in this realm are signed is irrelevant "because we have approximated to the state in which they were written" —the present theory accounts systematically for Forster's metaphorically expressed feelings by saying that to the extent one enters this realm, one has aesthetically re-created the proposition discovered initially by the artist and in this sense one approximates to the state in which the words were written.

I suggest that these are considerations which justify the use of such phrases as "the autonomous realm of art." The theory here presented consequently underwrites a paramount point of the doctrine of Art for Art's Sake. I shall conclude this chapter by showing that this characteristic of aesthetic experience is not incompatible with the Art for Life's Sake aspects of the theory adumbrated in section I above.

III. SYNTHESIS

Aesthetic experience of the propositional character of art objects, by involving the subjective aim of the experience, transports its subject into an autonomous realm. But the subject does not stay there forever; he returns to the realm of overarching subjective aims. These "worldly" aims, however, need not necessarily remain unchanged by the intervening aesthetic experience. An appetition, an aim after a goal, consists of both a physical and a conceptual feeling—in the case of thirst there is the feeling of dryness and the idea of quenching that dryness. The physical inheritance is, of course, crucial; what one aims at is conditioned by it. A man aiming at Wimbledon's center court breaks his wrist in an accident and can no longer play championship tennis; his "aim" alters. When a person experiences a work of art he enters the autonomous realm of art, but when he returns to his everyday life, that encounter with the art object remains with him as part of the inheritance that conditions his aims. Since an art object exerts a dynamic impact on consciousness (which emerges with great intensity in aesthetic experience as an element in the subjective form of a prehension which involves a proposition[4]), it follows that aesthetic experiences can be of great significance in the formulation of overarching aims. For example, it is not unreasonable to postulate that a college senior might read *Death of a Salesman* and *Point of No Return* in an English seminar and shortly thereafter abandon his intention of going on to business school in favor of a teaching career, and this largely as a result of aesthetic experiences which at their occurrence had cut off his everyday aims and transported him into the autonomous realm of art. There is in fact, then, no real conflict between Art for Art's Sake and Art for Life's Sake as those two doctrines are interpreted in the light of the present theory—the art object that grasps one aesthetically and unplugs one's experiences from overarching, worldly aims may, just because of its success in transporting persons into the realm of art, exert a powerful influence upon the reformulation of practical subjective aims. It would seem that every aesthetic theory would have to come to terms with the valid insights of the Iredell Jenkins and the Leo Tolstoys on the one hand and the Clive Bells and the Roger Frys on the other. It has been shown that the present theory is capable of such a synthesis.

4. See above, p. 62, and PR 372.

11. Conclusion

EARLY in Part II it was suggested that the initial points in the aesthetic analysis were like the first occurrence of a major theme in a symphony; it would be only after other themes had appeared and shared in the development that the opening motifs could reappear in their total significance. The initial theme was the doctrine that the work of art has the ontological status of a Whiteheadian proposition. This was further elaborated in the course of introducing the second theme, that aesthetic experience is experience, the subjective aim of which is to re-create the proposition objectified in the performance of a work of art. The development of the argument reached its climax when these two theories were interwoven with a third, that artistic creation is the qualification of dimly felt horizontal transmutations to logical subjects, bedded in specific artistic media, which mediate the contrast with actuality and hence articulate the dimly felt horizontal transmutations into conscious aesthetic awareness. Chapters 9 and 10 constitute a coda dwelling briefly on the questions of truth in art and the function of art. The significance of these five chapters, as I believe, lies not in this or that particular doctrine but in two major points, the first being the way the major themes each depend on the others and coalesce into one coherent scheme for interpreting the phenomena of the aesthetic life. Concrete examples from my personal experience and from that of artists and aes-

theticians have been cited to demonstrate the adequacy
of the present theory for interpreting the phenomena of
the aesthetic life. Secondly, the significance of these five
chapters is that the doctrines they expound emerge from
Whitehead's brilliant speculative account of the nature of
things. Plausible, I hope, in their own right, they gain additional stature, as well as clarity and precision, from their
association with metaphysical theory. Hulme, in his essay
"Bergson's Theory of Art," carefully assembles a group of
suppositions which he finds essential "for the purpose of
being able to convey over and state the nature of the activity you get in art." [1] Suddenly, feigning wide-eyed won-
derment, he discovers: "Now the extraordinary importance
of Bergson for any theory of art is that, starting with a different aim altogether, seeking merely to give an account of
reality, he arrives at certain conclusions as being true, and
these conclusions are the very things which we had to suppose in order to give an account of art." [2] In this book I
have substituted the philosophy of Whitehead for that of
Bergson, but I have retained Hulme's insight that only as
they are firmly grounded in a metaphysical theory are the
expressions one uses in aesthetic discourse "part of a definite conception of reality and not mere metaphors in-
vented especially for the purpose of describing art." [3]

It is also the case that the metaphysical system briefly
sketched in Chapters 2–4 grows in stature as the result
of sponsoring the aesthetic theory. Susanne Langer was
quoted in Chapter 1 to the effect that a philosophical
theory is judged not on the basis of "irrefutable proofs"
but on the basis of its ability to operate successfully with
concepts that give rise to insight and discovery. Hence my
aesthetic theory enhances Whitehead's metaphysical sys-

1. *Speculations,* p. 146.
2. Ibid.
3. Ibid., p. 169.

tem by demonstrating its applicability and adequacy within yet another dimension of human experience.[4] The mutual way in which the metaphysical system and the aesthetic analysis each add to the stature of the other binds Parts I and II of this book into a philosophical unity serving to strengthen the over-all appeal of Whitehead's philosophy of organism.

4. See above, p. 5.

Bibliography

Materials on Whitehead

BOOKS BY WHITEHEAD

Adventures of Ideas, New York, Macmillan, 1933.
The Function of Reason, Boston, Beacon Press, 1958.
Modes of Thought, New York, Macmillan, 1938.
The Principles of Natural Knowledge, Cambridge, England, University Press, 1919.
Process and Reality, New York, Macmillan, 1929.
Religion in the Making, Cambridge, England, University Press, 1926.
Science and the Modern World, New York, Macmillan, 1925.

ARTICLES ON WHITEHEAD

Johnson, A. H., "Whitehead's Theory of Actual Entities," *Philosophy of Science*, 12 (1945), 237–95.
Lowe, Victor, "The Development of Whitehead's Philosophy," in *The Philosophy of Alfred North Whitehead*, ed. Paul A. Schilpp (New York, Tudor Publishing Co., 1951), pp. 15–124.

BOOKS ON WHITEHEAD

Blyth, John W., *Whitehead's Theory of Knowledge*, Providence, Brown University, 1941.
Christian, William A., *An Interpretation of Whitehead's*

Metaphysics, New Haven, Yale University Press, 1959.

Leclerc, Ivor, *Whitehead's Metaphysics*, New York, Macmillan, 1958.

Schilpp, Paul Arthur, ed., *The Philosophy of Alfred North Whitehead*, New York, Tudor Publishing Co., 1951.

Stallknecht, Newton P., *Studies in the Philosophy of Creation*, Princeton, Princeton University Press, 1934.

Thompson, Edmund Jabez, *An Analysis of the Thought of Whitehead and Hocking Concerning Good and Evil*, Chicago, University of Chicago Press, 1935.

MATERIALS ON AESTHETICS

ARTICLES ON AESTHETICS

Bullough, Edward, "Psychical Distance as a Factor in Art and an Aesthetic Principle," *British Journal of Psychology*, 5 (1912), 87–118.

Cobb, John B., Jr., "Toward Clarity in Aesthetics," *Philosophy and Phenomenological Research*, 18 (1957), 169–89.

Greene, Theodore M., "The Scope of Aesthetics," *Journal of Aesthetics and Art Criticism*, 8 (1950), 221–28.

Hospers, John, "The Croce-Collingwood Theory of Art," *Philosophy*, 31 (1956), 291–308.

Lippincott, Gertrude, "A Dancer's Note to Aestheticians," *Journal of Aesthetics and Art Criticism*, 8 (1949), 97–105.

Morse, Marston, "Mathematics and the Arts," *Yale Review* (1951), pp. 604–12.

Shaw, Theodore L., "Art's Sleep Walkers" and "The Metropolitan Museum Lays an Egg" *Critical*, 1–4 (October 1959, November 1959, January 1960, April 1960). Boston, Stuart Publications.

Vivas, Eliseo, "A Definition of the Esthetic Experience," *Journal of Philosophy*, 34 (1937), 628–34.

Weitz, Morris, "The Role of Theory in Aesthetics," *Journal of Aesthetics and Art Criticism*, 15 (1956), 27–35.
Wimsatt, W. K., Jr., "The Domain of Criticism," *Journal of Aesthetics and Art Criticism*, 8 (1950), 213–20.

BOOKS ON AESTHETICS

Bell, Clive, *Art*, New York, Capricorn Books, Putnam, 1958.
Brooks, Cleanth, and Robert Penn Warren, *Understanding Poetry*, New York, Holt, rev. ed. 1955.
Collingwood, R. G., *The Principles of Art*, New York, Oxford University Press, Galaxy Book, 1958.
Croce, Benedetto, *Aesthetic*, New York, Noonday Press, 1958.
Delacroix, Henri, *Psychologie de l'Art*, Paris, Felix Alcan, 1927.
Dorner, Alexander, *The Way beyond "Art,"* 1st ed. New York, Wittenborn, Schultz, 1947; 2d ed. New York, New York University, 1958.
Ducasse, Curt John, *The Philosophy of Art*, New York, Lincoln Mac Veagh, Dial Press, 1929.
Forster, E. M., *Anonymity: An Enquiry*, London, Leonard and Virginia Woolf at the Hogarth Press, 1925.
Gardner, Helen, *Art Through The Ages*, New York, Harcourt, Brace, 1948.
Gasset, Ortega y, *The Dehumanization of Art and Other Writings on Art and Culture*, Garden City, Doubleday, 1956.
Greene, Theodore M., *The Arts and the Art of Criticism*, Princeton, Princeton University Press, 1940.
———*The Meaning of the Humanities*, Princeton, Princeton University Press, 1940.
Hanslick, Eduard, *The Beautiful in Music*, New York, Liberal Arts Press, 1957.

Hulme, T. E., *Speculations,* New York, Harcourt, Brace, 1924.

Jenkins, Iredell, *Art and the Human Enterprise,* Cambridge, Harvard University Press, 1958.

Kandinsky, Wassily, *Concerning the Spiritual in Art,* New York, Wittenborn, Schultz, 1947.

Langer, Susanne K., *Reflections on Art,* Baltimore, Johns Hopkins University Press, 1958.

Lee, Vernon, *Music and Its Lovers,* London, George Allen and Unwin, 1932.

Maritain, Jacques, *Creative Intuition In Art and Poetry,* New York, Meridian Books, 1957.

Munro, Thomas, *Towards Science in Aesthetics,* New York, Liberal Arts Press, 1956.

Nahm, Milton, *The Artist as Creator,* Baltimore, Johns Hopkins University Press, 1956.

Panofsky, Erwin, *Meaning in the Visual Arts,* Garden City, Doubleday, 1955.

——*The Life and Art of Albrecht Durer,* Princeton, Princeton University Press, 1955.

Pepper, Stephen C., *Aesthetic Quality,* New York, Scribner's, 1937.

Rich, D. C., *Seurat and the Evolution of "La Grande Jatte,"* Chicago, University of Chicago Press, 1935.

Santayana, George, *The Sense of Beauty,* New York, Modern Library, 1955.

Vivas, Eliseo, and Murray Kreiger, *The Problems of Aesthetics,* New York, Rinehart, 1953.

Weitz, Morris, *Problems in Aesthetics,* New York, Macmillan, 1959.

Wellek, René, and Austin Warren, *Theory of Literature,* New York, Harcourt, Brace, 1949.

Wimsatt, W. K., Jr., *The Verbal Icon,* New York, Noonday Press, 1958.

MISCELLANEOUS MATERIALS

Bevan, Edwyn, *Symbolism and Belief*, Boston, Beacon Press Paperback, 1957.

Bracker, Milton, "The 'Quietly Overwhelming' Robert Frost," *New York Times Magazine* (November 30, 1958), pp. 15, 57, 59, 62.

Cassirer, Ernst, *An Essay on Man*, New Haven, Yale University Press, 1944.

Cornford, Francis M., *Plato's Cosmology*, London, Routledge and Kegan Paul, 1937.

Frost, Robert, *Complete Poems of Robert Frost*, New York, Holt, 1949.

Hume, David, *An Abstract of a Treatise of Human Nature*, published as a supplement to *An Inquiry Concerning Human Understanding*, New York, Liberal Arts Press, 1955.

James, William, *The Varieties of Religious Experience*, New York, New American Library of World Literature, 1958.

——*Some Problems of Philosophy*, New York, Longmans, Green, 1948.

Myhill, John, "Some Philosophical Implications of Mathematical Logic," *Review of Metaphysics*, 6 (1952), 165–98.

Spencer, Herbert, *Principles of Psychology*, New York, Appleton, 1871.

Index

Abstraction, and intellectuality, 62
Actual entity: *formaliter*, 32 n., 104; *objectivé*, 140; and process, 9; self-creation of, 46
Actual occasions. *See* Actual entity
Aesthetic, the, 156; in Cobb's theory, 134–42
  aesthetic attention, in music, 150–53. *See also* Attention
  aesthetic experience, 118–19, 134–59; as aesthetic re-creation, 144, 146, 148–49, 158, 179; and beauty, 144–45, 147; and meaning, 158–59; and objectified propositions, 146; and propositions, 143; and subjective aim, 118–19, 143, 200–1; and subjective form, 143; theory of author, 142–45
  aesthetic harmony, 137
  aesthetic theory: characteristics of, 101–2; clarity and precision in, 3–4; extent of, 6, 95–96; as reflecting back upon metaphysics, 4–5; as requiring metaphysics, 3–4; Whitehead's own investigations, 5–6
Agency, 9
Ambiguity, the process-product, 101
Appearance: and reality, 186–92; as sense perception, 187
Architecture, 128–29, 132
Aristotle, 194
Armstrong, Louis, 129–30

Art: boundaries of, 126–27; function of, 193–202; immortality of, 124–26; as language, 150; realm of, 199–201; and truth, 185–92
  abstract art, and burlesque, 156–57; and music, 157
  Art for Art's Sake, 116–17, 190, 192, 195, 199–201
  Art for Life's Sake, 116, 192–93, 195–98
  art objects: generality of, 132–33; as lures for feeling, 124; as independent of artist's mind, 179–80; ontological status of, 98–133 passim; not physical artifact, 179–80; as propositions, 146, 148; and subjective aim, 124
  artistic creation, 35, 160–84; and the conceived medium, 172; as discovery, 180–84; and God, 180–84; God and reversions in, 181–84; and horizontal transmutation, 166; and mathematics, 167, 167 n.; and metaphysics, 160–61; in nonperformer arts, 176–77; and the physical medium, 170–73; the problem of, 168; and reversions, 181–84
  artistic expression, 167–70; and externalization, 173; and horizontal transmutation, 168,

mode of presentational immediacy, 82–87, 136, 143; and complex societies, 83; limitations of, 85

Performance, as objectified proposition, 107

Performer: and artist, 173–78; more than technician, 174–75

Performer arts, and nonperformer arts, 98, 130–32

Perspective, 48

Philosophical theory, excellence of, 4–5. *See also* Metaphysical theory

Physical pole, 51

Physical purpose, 55, 83; and propositions, 57; and propositional prehensions (feelings), 64–65, 167–68

Physical recognition, 66

Picasso, Pablo, 189

Plato, 40, 95, 160–61, 166

Plummer, Christopher, 121–22

Poetry, analysis of ontological status of, 99–100

Pollock, Jackson, 129

Potentiality. *See* Eternal objects, and potentiality

Prehensions (feelings): conceptual, 43, 50–52, 102–7; mutual, 73–74, 76, 78 n.; negative, 49; strain, 85, 87; theory of, 27

intellectual, 65–69; and conscious perceptions, 66; and intuitive judgments, 66

physical, 43, 102–7; as composing first phase of concrescence, 47; hybrid, 43; simple, 47; two subphases, 47–48

propositional, 56, 102–7; authentic perceptive, 67–69; direct authentic perceptive, 69; imaginative, 66; perceptive, 66; and physical purpose, 167–68; and propositions, 105; unauthentic perceptive, 67–69

Presentational immediacy. *See* Per-

ception, mode of presentational immediacy

Process: and actual entities, 9; macroscopic, 22–23; microscopic, 22–23; microscopic fundamental? 22; as *one*, 22–23; relation of two senses of, 21–23

Projection. *See* Sensa

Propositions, 46; and aesthetic experience, 143; as datum for consciousness, 62–63; definition of, 56; and horizontal transmutations, 171; as independent of propositional feelings, 105–7; logical subject of, 56–57, 64 and 104 (as abstraction), 103–7, 111–12 (in art), 168; and logicians, 106, 122–24, 126, 171, 185–86; as lures for feeling, 106, 171–72; and physical purposes, 57, 64–65; predicative pattern of, 56–57, 103–7; primary function of, 185–86; and propositional prehensions, 105; theory of, 102–7

Psychical distance, 98, 108–12, 148; and propositional character of art, 109

Reality, and appearance, 186–92

Reason, as countertendency, 196

Region, 83

Reiteration, resistance to, 125; and beauty, 159

Reversion, conceptual, 51–53, 81; in artistic creation, 181–84; double, 60–61

Rich, D. C., 130

Saroyan, William, 120–21

Satisfaction, 69–71, 140, 197; genetic analysis of, 47; intensity of, and societies, 80

Sensa: and contemporary regions, 83; donation of, 83, 87 n.; enhancement of, 83, 86; as eternal

Wellek, René, 98–101, 118

Whitehead, A. N.: extent of his own aesthetic concern, 5–7; theory of beauty 6, 155–56; theory of the function of art, 193–94

Wimsatt, W. K., Jr., 96, 100

Wolf, Hugo, 129–30, 174, 177

Wright, Frank Lloyd, 128

Zeno, 12